WARP SPEED

WARP SPEED

INSIDE THE OPERATION THAT BEAT
COVID, **THE CRITICS**, AND **THE ODDS**

PAUL MANGO

REPUBLIC
BOOK PUBLISHERS

WARP SPEED

First Edition

ISBN (Hardcover 9781645720546) (ebook 9781645720553)

For inquiries about volume orders, please contact:

Republic Book Publishers

27 West 2oth Street

Suite 1103

New York NY 10011

editor@republicbookpublishers.com

Published in the United States by Republic Book Publishers

Distributed by Independent Publishers Group

www.ipgbook.com

Book designed by Mark Karis

Printed in the United States of America

CONTENTS

FOREWORD BY

SEN. TOM COTTON

China gave the world the Wuhan coronavirus pandemic. America developed the vaccines to end it.

Warp Speed tells the remarkable story of Operation Warp Speed, the crash effort to produce the Covid-19 vaccines. Few people can tell the story as ably as Paul Mango since he played a leading role in Operation Warp Speed from the very beginning.

I've known Paul for years as a friend and trusted advisor. He served his country in the Army, succeeded in business, and then ran for governor of Pennsylvania in 2018. While I was disappointed that Paul came up just short in the primary, Pennsylvania's loss was America's gain. Paul subsequently went to work for the Department of Health and Human Services, where his leadership, management skills, and strategic vision contributed directly to Operation Warp Speed's success.

This success wasn't by chance, and it wasn't a miracle. Like the Manhattan Project and the Apollo Program before it, Operation Warp Speed was the product of hard work and a brilliant team coming together to do the near impossible: develop a vaccine, test it, get it approved, get it produced, get it distributed, and get it in arms—all in less than a year while the pandemic raged.

The success of Operation Warp Speed is even more remarkable given the sheer number of mistakes and inaccurate predictions made by the public-health bureaucracy during this crisis. Despite their overweening self-confidence and self-regard, the public-health "experts" seemed to get everything wrong when it counted—and that's if they could make up their minds at all. First, they told us that masks don't work. Then they told us that masks are mandatory, then optional, then mandatory again. By the time you read this book, the guidance may have changed yet again—and not based on scientific evidence, but on political fads. These so-called experts also advocated for protracted lockdowns that resulted in the sharpest economic contraction in American history, destroying the livelihoods and dreams of millions of Americans. They then stubbornly fought every attempt to lift these restrictions and give us back our freedom. At the time of writing, the public-health bureaucracy is still working with their cronies in the teachers' unions to keep kids out of the classroom, despite clear evidence showing that it is safe for them to return.

Unsurprisingly, many of these same experts scoffed at Operation Warp Speed. Talking heads on CNN, ABC and MSNBC derided the possibility that a vaccine could be approved on an accelerated timeline. After all, they said, no vaccine in history had been developed in under four years. Some fatalistically predicted a coronavirus vaccine could take as long as a decade.

These skeptics were wrong. They may have known the long odds, but they didn't know Paul Mango and the extraordinary team that President Trump had assembled.

I asked a high-level pharmaceutical executive directly involved in Operation Warp Speed if this program could have happened under a different administration. His answer was unequivocal: "No." The Trump administration was willing to take risks, create precedents, slice through red tape and other bureaucratic Gordian knots, and do whatever was necessary to develop safe and effective vaccines in record time. An administration made of weaker stuff would have hidden behind "process," lowered expectations, and generally moved at a much slower pace. It speaks to the leadership of President Trump and the patriotism of the men and women of Operation Warp Speed that they rejected these excuses and charged ahead.

Ultimately, Operation Warp Speed is not just an extraordinary technical achievement. It's a testament to American ingenuity and greatness. We should learn from its success and build on its achievement.

INTRODUCTION

"WE HAVE A PROBLEM IN CHINA."

On Friday, January 3, 2020, Dr. Robert Redfield, director of the Centers for Disease Control and Prevention, phoned Alex Azar, secretary of the Department of Health and Human Services (HHS) and with those words, "We have a problem in China," broke to the secretary and those of us on his immediate staff news that was about to change the entire world. Neither he, nor any other expert, knew much at that time about the characteristics of the virus that would become known formally as SARS-CoV2, but he knew enough to sense that we needed to respond, and respond quickly. The virus, which originated in Wuhan, was already showing up in other Chinese cities and likely gestating in countries that did business with China, meaning every significant economy in the world. Early indications pointed to a pathogen that could be as deadly as the one that caused the World War I–era Spanish Flu, which infected half a billion people globally in 1918–1919 and killed at least 50 million.[1]

Thus began an odyssey of pandemic response actions, strategies, and regulatory processes that would consume the department of Health and Human Services (HHS), along with much of the administration, until inauguration day 2021. Only one of these responses, Operation Warp Speed, which delivered more safe and effective vaccines more quickly than almost all of the world's experts thought possible, has been universally acclaimed as a resounding success. This did not happen by accident.

Shortly after the call from Dr. Redfield, the assistant secretary for Preparedness and Response at HHS, Dr. Bob Kadlec, activated the Disaster Leadership Group to assess the healthcare system's capacity and resilience, to determine supply chain readiness, and to initiate work on "medical countermeasures" (i.e., vaccines, therapeutics, and diagnostics). The administration's initial strategy in response to a potential pandemic was to attempt to contain the virus in China, and this led initially to a screening process for anyone entering the country from Wuhan and was followed in late January by the president's imposition of an outright travel ban from China. When the strategy of containment proved insufficient, we moved on to mitigation (e.g., social distancing, washing of hands, masking) designed to inhibit the spread of the virus in the United States. When this strategy proved insufficient, we moved on to one of effectively absorbing the surges of hospitalized COVID patients in concentrated geographies such as the tristate area around New York City. In support of this, the administration mobilized the private sector to manufacture tens of thousands of additional ventilators and millions of articles of personal protective equipment (PPE). Because of the logistical requirements associated with distributing these goods, FEMA, the Federal Emergency Management Administration, was activated on March 19, 2020, as the federal government's lead agency in the pandemic response.

Several weeks into this series of inadequate attempts to "get out in front" of the virus, two characteristics about SARS-CoV2 came into focus and altered our perspective completely. First, that this virus was spreading asymptomatically (i.e., persons who were infected had no symptoms yet were infecting others) and second, that its clinical impact on humans was asymmetric (i.e., it would kill some within days, but cause nothing more than sniffles in others). This is when our imperative became clear: the only effective remedy to controlling this virus and its destructive impact on lives and the economy would be to develop and manufacture hundreds of millions of doses of safe and effective vaccines as quickly as possible.

At this point, the Trump administration—and the Azar team in particular—had already begun evolving what, in the end, would prove the world's most innovative and effective response to the crisis: the record-time research, development, mass production, universal distribution, and administration of a set of highly effective vaccines against the disease. Before the year was out, the public-private partnership that we dubbed "Operation Warp Speed" was delivering two distinct COVID vaccines throughout the nation. One additional Warp Speed vaccine received approval and was in use by early 2021.

Operation Warp Speed was the most successful emergency vaccine development and deployment effort ever, and the most successful biomedical public–private partnership in history. Internationally, China and Russia tried to match us and failed. They produced inferior inoculations. By July 2021, their hopes of scoring global propaganda were backfiring. Stories were appearing about the "collapse of Moscow and Beijing vaccine diplomacy."[2]

To put Warp Speed's performance in perspective, think of when Roger Bannister ran the first four-minute mile. That was 1954. Today, sixty-eight years later, the record is not much changed at three minutes, forty-three seconds. If we equate today's record mile to the previous record for vaccine development, then Warp Speed's performance would be the equivalent of running the mile in forty-five seconds, an 80 percent improvement.

How do we measure the value of this speed?

In lives? A National Institutes of Health-sponsored study published in Health Affairs on August 18, 2021 asserts that the three Operation Warp Speed Vaccines saved approximately 140,000 lives during their first six months of use alone, from December 2020 until May 2021.[3] As of this writing, each of the Warp Speed vaccines appears to be effective against some, and maybe all, variants, meaning that the variant-caused uptick in cases will translate into far fewer deaths.[4] As of November 2021 nearly all COVID deaths (98 percent) were among the unvaccinated.[5]

Or in dollars? University of Chicago economists and veterans of the Trump Council of Economic Advisors Casey B. Mulligan and Tomas J. Philipson recently estimated that "accelerating the arrival of the vaccines by six months was worth $1.8 trillion to the US economy—and more to the rest of the world."[6] Those dollars translated into thousands of stores, restaurants, and small business that could keep their doors open and, throughout the economy, to hundreds of thousands, perhaps multiple millions, of jobs saved or restored.

Many in the media have attributed this success to some sort of unnamed "miracle"; a *deus ex machina* arbitrarily introduced to unravel the mysteries of vaccine development, the vagaries of biological manufacturing, and the logistical complexities of distribution. Others attribute it to good fortune.[7]

The core members of the Warp Speed team bristle at these suggestions of miracles and luck. They know that Operation Warp Speed was not as much a scientific miracle as it was a meticulously designed initiative. Success was the result of a deliberate strategy, exacting execution, an exceptional team that worked together exceptionally well, a unique public-private partnership—and a president's and secretary's remarkable leadership. It overcame media melodrama, outside political manipulation, internal squabbles, and unprecedented logistical hurdles to produce what for many outsiders was unimaginable success in the middle of a pandemic that had all but paralyzed the entire world.

Some say we achieved success at the expense of safety. This could not be further from the truth. The minimum number of enrollees in the Warp Speed clinical trials as specified by the FDA was half again larger than normal vaccine trials. The interval of time from when the median trial participant received his second dose until the FDA would grant an emergency use authorization was extended beyond that of previous trials. All other required steps and criteria were those of normal trials. Indeed, Peter Marks, who leads the FDA's vaccine approval unit, restructured his team and its internal processes to work around the clock to accelerate the evaluations. So while the *process* of evaluation was restructured not a single *standard* of evaluation was compromised. In fact, the standards for approval in many ways were more stringent than those used in normal evaluations.

There were five simple keys to Operation Warp Speed's success. First, both vaccines that reached the country before year's end—Pfizer/BioNTech's and Moderna's—took advantage of genetic techniques that had been under development for more than a decade but had not previously been applied to vaccine development. Nonetheless, the Operation Warp Speed team had confidence in their potential and made substantial investments in their ultimate success. The advancements represented by the mRNA technology platform enabled vaccine design to be finished in days, not months or years, as in the past.

The second key was performing in parallel tasks that were typically performed in series: reserving, equipping, and activating factories to fill massive orders of vaccine doses, vials, and injection supplies, developing and making specialized packaging, lining up shippers early (FedEx and UPS), as well as setting up tens of thousands of neighborhood sites for administering the shots (CVS, Walgreens, and many others) *before* the clinical trials revealed whether or not any vaccine would be safe and effective. The federal government assumed the financial risk associated with this in ways that would have been prohibitive for companies like Moderna.

The third was selecting vaccine candidates for investment in ways that spread our risk as a venture capitalist would over a variety of technologies and companies. We understood that some might fail, but we needed only one to be successful. Some did fail, but the successes delivered spectacular returns.

The fourth was designing a governance structure that bypassed the slow grind of bureaucratic decision-making. We created a board comprising only the essential players from HHS, the DoD, and the White House. This board reported directly to the president. Decisions on vaccine candidate selection, resources, and distribution strategies were made in hours and days rather than weeks and months.

The fifth and last key was a leadership philosophy comprising three fundamental beliefs: first, delegate key tasks to those who possess the most knowledge and experience rather than to those who have lofty titles. This included bringing in experts from the private sector where the government lacked the talent. Second, that the impact derived from collaboration and teamwork far exceeds that derived from individual talent. Debating differences of opinion was encouraged, but undermining the integrity of teamwork was not to be tolerated. Third, rigorously prevent the federal government from engaging in any activities the private sector could perform better. This last belief led to a very unique public-private partnership. The government provided the resources, clarity of objective, and the regulatory context for success. America's private sector brought its ingenuity and innovative spirit to the table. The result was delivering more vaccines to America, and the world, in less time than had ever been done at any time in the history of biomedicine. The federal government *enabled* success, America's private sector *delivered* it.

Neither the government nor industry could have done all this alone. Left to themselves government's existing agencies could not have done it at all. In Operation Warp Speed we assembled and mobilized an unorthodox mix of government and private industry expertise and resources—and saved hundreds of thousands, maybe millions of lives.

Designing the vaccine itself proved the easy part. The bigger hurdles were actually manufacturing it, guiding it through trials and regulatory approval, producing hundreds of millions of doses, putting them into vials, and moving the vials along with syringes and needles to places in every community in the nation where trained health workers were ready to begin administering the doses to every willing arm by the end of 2020. That was our goal.

But smooth and efficient as it may appear in retrospect, Operation Warp Speed was not destined for inevitable success. Scientific, manufacturing, and logistical hurdles were only the start of our challenges. Operation Warp Speed had to overcome the obstacles, criticisms, and tensions that emerge when members of the media and others who are politically motivated are eager to attack and disparage *any* initiative undertaken by a president, when the country is in the middle of a politically motivated presidential campaign, and when humans with oversized egos are involved.

Even so, eleven months after the posting of COVID-19 virus's genetic sequence, the Food and Drug Administration granted emergency use authorizations (EUA) to Pfizer-BioNTech (December 11) and Moderna (December 16) for their vaccines. On December 14, Sandra Lindsey, a nurse in Long Island Jewish Medical Center's intensive care unit, received the first post-authorized inoculation.[8] By New Year's Eve, 2.8 million Americans had been given at least one dose of the two-dose shots,[9] growing to 25 million at the end of January. By the Spring of 2021, any American desiring a vaccine could get one. Despite the FDA's guideline that vaccines be at least 50 percent effective, those first two vaccines, Pfizer-BioNTech and Moderna, were rated at a near-unprecedented 95 percent and 94.5 percent effective, respectively.

One of the earliest examples of media pessimism and poorly informed experts was an April 30 *New York Times* article by Stuart Thompson. This was at a time when we were still formalizing the team that would eventually comprise Operation Warp Speed.

Referring to predictions about having a vaccine in 18 months and editorializing at the start that "the grim truth behind this rosy forecast is that a vaccine probably won't arrive anytime soon," Mr. Thompson then quoted Dr. Peter Hotez, dean of the National School of Tropical Medicine at the Baylor College of Medicine saying, "If you want to make the 18-month timeframe, one way to do it is to put as many horses in the race as you can."[10] In fact, our ultimately successful strategy of focusing on a relatively small number of vaccine candidates eligible for US government support was nearly the opposite of Dr. Hotez's assertion.

We intentionally *limited* the slate of candidates to the six most likely to succeed. Dr. Moncef Slaoui, our chief scientific advisor, and GEN Gus Perna, our logistics lead, understood the basic management principle that too many priorities would dilute management time and attention and critical resources such as raw materials and manufacturing equipment, challenge clinical trial enrollment, and greatly complicate the vaccine distribution and administration task.

Moving on, Thompson quoted the head of vaccine manufacturing at Merck, saying that "the manufacturing task is insurmountable" (he was actually right as it applied to Merck), and a Canadian vaccine policy expert who predicted we would not see a vaccine approved until at least 2021 or 2022, adding, "This is very optimistic and of relatively low probability."

Just two weeks later one of the best examples of how *absolutely wrong* the so-called "experts" were comes from an interview conducted on the very day of the Operation Warp Speed Rose Garden kick-off on May 15, 2020. It occurred during that evening's broadcast of *The 11th Hour with Brian Williams*. Williams was interviewing Dr. Irwin Redlener of Columbia University. Dr. Redlener founded the National Center for Disaster Preparedness and was the director of the Pandemic Response and Recovery Initiative.

Williams asked whether it was possible to have a vaccine by the end of 2020. Dr. Redlener responded, "Oh Brian, you know, what's another day of POTUS in Wonderland here?" He later added, "It is impossible to get that done by the end of the year."[11] Williams robotically nodded.

Pessimism turned to cynicism when in June 2020, Dr. Ezekiel Emanuel, architect of President Barack Obama's Affordable Care Act, co-authored a *New York Times* op-ed headlined, "Could Trump Turn a Vaccine into a Campaign Stunt?" with a subtitle, "In a desperate search for a boost, he could release a coronavirus vaccine that has not been shown to be safe and effective as an October surprise."[12]

Politicizing the development of a safe and effective vaccine in the midst of a presidential campaign did not help either. In September, Democratic Party presidential nominee Joe Biden said of our work, "I trust vaccines. I trust scientists. But I do not trust Donald Trump. And at this moment the American people can't either."[13] Later Senator Kamala Harris chimed in that if President Trump assured the nation that a vaccine was safe, she "would not take his word for it."[14]

These professions of doubt did not stop either Mr. Biden or Ms. Harris from getting their first doses within days of FDA authorization (on December 21,[15] one week after Pfizer received its EUA for the president-elect and on December 29[16] for the vice president-elect). But by then they had helped to instigate doubts that have left too many Americans reluctant to receive the vaccine—reluctance that Mr. Biden later attempted to combat with mandates and sanctions.

Some of the more disappointing and disingenuous criticisms we faced came from members of the Biden transition team itself. In November of 2020 attempting to facilitate a seamless transition during a global pandemic, we set aside scores of offices and conference room space inside the Department of Health and Human Services headquarters where the Operation Warp Speed team was also located for those in the new administration who would assume leadership of the operation. They then chose not to show up. Yes, we conducted videoconferences with them, but not a single transition team member showed up in person. Not once. Apparently, they were concerned about the possibility of COVID transmission. One can only imagine what the Warp Speed team, many of whose members were combat veterans and all of whom (both military and civilian) had shown up *every day* in person for the prior seven months thought of this. The Warp Speed team members considered it a matter of duty to be present regardless of the potential for personal harm. Then shortly after the inauguration of the new president, members of the transition team and others in the administration complained to the media that we had "no plan," left them a "mess" and that they had to "start from scratch." Really? How would they have known?

The spectrum of politicians, media pontificators, and especially scientists who should have known better, claiming with certainty that the Trump administration would *not* have a safe and effective vaccine before the end of the calendar year 2020, or even soon thereafter, was astonishing and irresponsible. Indeed, has there ever been a US government initiative for which so many were so completely wrong on so many dimensions?

But beyond the *external* pressure created by a clearly biased media, ill-informed "experts," and pandering political candidates resided three sets of tensions *internal* to the Operation Warp Speed team, all of which required constant attention and vigilance.

The first of these was tension between Dr. Moncef Slaoui, our chief scientific advisor, and the white house coronavirus task force coordinator, Dr. Deb Birx. Dr. Slaoui was insistent that we needed to mitigate major development and manufacturing risks by advancing six vaccine candidates across three different technology platforms. This was the venture capital mindset we mentioned earlier. Dr. Birx was just as insistent that we focus almost exclusively on only one of these three platforms, a tried-and-tested technology referred to as "protein sub-unit" being utilized by two of our vaccine candidate companies, Novovax and Sanofi. As of November 2021, neither of these two companies' vaccines had received an Emergency Use Authorization (EUA) from the FDA. She was not only wrong, but in the process of asserting her perspectives she denigrated the members of the Warp Speed team in ways that became intolerable.

A second source of tension emerged between the leaders of the Army

Material Command and the CDC represented principally by Dr. Nancy Messionier, Director of the National Center for Immunization and Respiratory Diseases. Dr. Messionier had a strong preference for using the nation's public health agencies to both distribute and administer the vaccine doses. The Army team, led by GEN Gus Perna, which had been supporting combat operations in the Middle East for nearly two decades, had a strong preference for using the more nimble, innovative private sector partners for these tasks. We eventually chose the private sector, and these partners wound up performing their tasks nearly flawlessly.

The third source of tension arose between the entire Operation Warp Speed team and Pfizer. Of all the companies in which we invested, Pfizer was both the least transparent and least collaborative. It would not let us observe its manufacturing processes for months and then failed to deliver the contracted amounts of doses it promised in November and December of 2020. This eroded the credibility of GEN Perna's distribution team in the eyes of many governors.

Again, Warp Speed was not as much a scientific miracle as it was a deliberate, strategically sound, meticulously designed initiative. Its leaders faced a broad spectrum of obstacles and challenges both from within and without. It never really *eliminated* these obstacles and threats to its success. Many of them persisted until the end. Rather, it *overcame* these obstacles with an impressive array of ingenuity, hard work, perseverance, principle, and resilience. An early example of this resilience occurred in April 2020 at the White House just as we were organizing the operation. When Secretary Azar shared the Warp Speed concept with White House Chief of Staff Mark Meadows for the first time, Mark's observation was, "Alex, if this fails, you will be blamed. If it is successful, you will not get the credit."[17] Azar's response was, "I can live with that."

How prescient.

1

FIRST STEPS

The starting gun in the global race for an effective and widely available COVID vaccine was fired on Friday, January 10, 2020. That day, a heroic (and later punished) Chinese virology team led by Yong-Zhen Zhang of Shanghai's Fudan University, working through Professor Edward Holmes of Australia's University of Sydney, posted the virus's genetic sequence on a global public health site, Virological.org.[1] By Monday night, January 13, the American pharmaceutical development firm, Moderna, using mRNA, a breakthrough genetic engineering technology, had designed a vaccine.[2] Scientists at Pfizer's research partner, BioNTech, did the same not much after that.

January 10, the day that the virus's genetic sequence became globally available, was also the day China reported its first COVID death. A little over a week later, January 20, China reported its first documented human-to-human COVID transmission. On the same day, the World Health Organization (WHO) reported the first documented cases outside China, in Japan, South Korea, and Thailand.[3] The next day the first US case came to light: a man in his thirties who had just returned from Wuhan. Ten days after that, January 31, President Trump shut down all travel of non-Americans from China (prompting charges of "xenophobia" from his critics[4]). Four days after that, February 4, the National Institutes of Health began testing the Moderna vaccine on mice.

Over the course of these days and weeks, Secretary Azar, our staff, along with thousands of other officials and medical experts throughout the nation and the world, sought insight into a number of critical questions: how deadly was this virus, how easily was it transmitted, what were the symptoms, could we contain it overseas, were we prepared to deal with it effectively in the US if we could not contain it? During this time, we at HHS were equally focused on repatriating and quarantining thousands of Americans arriving back from China, Japan, and those floating on pleasure ships in the middle of the ocean.

As the first identifiable COVID-19 US cases not a result of travel to China appeared in Washington State and Northern California in early February,[5] we began to understand the futility of attempting to contain the spread of the virus and began to assume the steps necessary to *mitigate* it, meaning limiting its spread rather than trying to prevent it from entering the country.

Not yet knowing the full extent of the virus's asymptomatic transmission, these early mitigation steps focused on identifying what were some of the obvious symptoms of those who were suspected to be infected: fever, coughing, and difficulty breathing. It was only a couple of weeks later, in early March, as the virus was spreading through parts of southern Europe with deadly consequences, and the realization that cases were likely entering the US not only from Asia but from Italy,

Spain, and other European countries, that the US began introducing much more stringent mitigation measures.

On March 6, President Trump signed the Coronavirus Preparedness and Response Supplemental Appropriations Act committing, among other funding, $826 million to the development of vaccines, therapeutics, and diagnostics and another $3.1 billion for activities including the development of vaccines.[6] On March 16, the NIH began human testing of the Moderna vaccine.[7]

The virus had been characterized scarcely nine weeks earlier. Having a vaccine ready for human testing so quickly had never transpired before.[8] It was a hopeful sign at a desperate moment. Across the nation, people were being urged to stay home. Places of public gathering—stores, restaurants, movie theaters, sports arenas—were closing. The US economy was beginning to shut down. One notable hot spot, the tristate metropolitan area around New York City, was exploding with new cases.[9]

This led to our posture evolving again from simply imposing stringent mitigation measures to doing everything possible to absorb the surge of COVID-19 patients. We needed more ventilators, more personal protective equipment including N95 masks, more gowns, more face shields, and more gloves. Hospitals in the NYC area were being overrun with COVID-19 patients, and they were ordering supplemental mobile refrigerators to be used as temporary morgues.[10]

By late March, with a better understanding of how the virus spread and how it affected individuals very, very differently, we began to understand that there were only two ways the pandemic would end: by achieving natural immunity with immense loss of life, or by achieving vaccinated immunity. Even the most optimistic estimates by the world's leading experts at the time thought developing and manufacturing a safe and effective vaccine would require more than a year and a half.[11]

Several weeks into the pandemic, there were a number of disparate yet important efforts underway within HHS. As early as January 10, when the NIH received the COVID viral DNA sequence from China,

HHS began to evaluate and invest in COVID-related vaccines and therapeutics. Peter Marks at the FDA had started screening approximately 100 potential vaccine candidates. However, there was little structure, integration, or joint governance of these efforts.

This all changed early one evening in late March 2020, shortly after the president ordered a national shutdown. A couple of us were in secretary Azar's office (which was usually the case near the end of the day) when we received a message that Alex Gorsky, the CEO of Johnson & Johnson (J&J), wished to speak to the secretary. Coincidentally, Gorsky was a good friend of mine from West Point, and was my wife's classmate there.

We patched Gorsky in. He thanked the secretary for permitting the Biomedical Advanced Research and Development Authority (BARDA) earlier that day to make a $450 million investment in the further development of J&J's vaccine.[12] The secretary acknowledged Gorsky's gratitude and, after a couple of niceties, concluded the call. The only complication was that neither Azar nor I, nor anyone else in the Chief of Staff's office, had known anything about this investment.

Shortly after the call, the secretary asked us to assemble the leadership team of the Biomedical Advanced Research and Development Authority (BARDA), an organization within HHS. He asked its members to describe what we were getting in return from J&J for this extraordinary investment. Essentially, the answer was "nothing." J&J planned on beginning its phase 1 clinical trial in September (six months away at the time). We were in the middle of a global pandemic, and such timing reflected a "business as usual" mindset on the part of our colleagues, which was unacceptable. This episode became the impetus for what eventually became Operation Warp Speed.

We soon found that too many industry players, as well as members of our own BARDA team, did not share the sense of urgency, financial risk tolerance, or the imagination consistent with what was rapidly becoming a difficult-to-mitigate, tragically consequential pandemic.

Having come from the pharmaceutical sector, Azar instinctively knew we needed to alter the status quo. We needed to infuse the department with external talent—experts from inside the vaccine development and manufacturing community who commanded great respect and possessed deep relationships. We would need to acquire logistics and contracting support, a role subsequently fulfilled by the Department of Defense. The federal government would need to bear the financial risks associated with accelerating timelines—financial risk that most pharmaceutical companies could not normally shoulder on their own. And we needed to establish a governance structure that overcame the glacial pace at which most official bureaucracies make decisions. Finally, we would need to *enable,* not act as a substitute for, the private sector innovation and dynamism necessary to develop, manufacture, distribute, and administer safe and effective vaccines in the little time we had.

Collectively, this shattering of the status quo in the government gave us a solid foundation for building our public-private partnership—a remarkable collaboration that would develop, manufacture, ship, and administer hundreds of millions of doses of multiple totally new vaccines in one-fifth the previous best time in the history of vaccine development.[13]

Shortly after the call from Gorsky and the subsequent meeting with BARDA, Azar formed an ad hoc advisory committee, the first meeting of which occurred on April 5. Attending this meeting were Dr. Francis Collins (director, National Institute of Health), Dr. Stephen Hahn (commissioner, Food and Drug Administration), Dr. Anthony Fauci (director, National Institute of Allergies and Infectious Diseases), Dr. Rick Bright (director, Biomedical Advanced Research and Development Authority), Dr. Janet Woodcock (director, Center for Drug Evaluation and Research), Dr. Robert Redfield (director, Centers for Disease Control and Prevention), Dr. Robert Kadlec (assistant secretary of HHS for Preparedness and Response), Azar, a few others from within the agencies, and me. We had a follow-up meeting of this group on April 8. Azar and I walked away from these two meetings with the impression that our internal team was acting too passively. We decided that we needed to accelerate the development of a vaccine through more active engagement of the pharmaceutical sector and more planning that included relevant industries.

On April 10, Azar, Kadlec, Peter Marks (director, Center for Biologics Evaluation and Research), and I met. Marks and Kadlec laid out the unprecedented progress of the pharmaceutical companies in designing what their scientists believed would prove effective vaccines against COVID. If they were right, Marks and Kadlec thought, there might be an accelerated path to vaccine development and deployment, that is, to moving from research to trials, to regulatory approval, to manufacturing, to shipping, finally to administering one or more vaccines throughout the nation before year's end. But if it was going to work, they said, we needed to get preparations for manufacturing started as soon as possible. Azar told them to plan as if they "were limited only by science and physics"—in other words, do not worry about money or manpower; he would supply them. It was at this meeting that Azar first used his initial moniker for the operation: "Manhattan Project 2."

All of us met again on April 13, and Dr. Marks presented the plan. We believed at that point a safe and effective vaccine manufactured at scale would be possible by the end of 2020, if everything went exactly right. It was during this meeting that Azar realized we would need to bring in talent from outside the department and the government. Almost immediately, he began talking up the concept and taking soundings on staffing it.

Later that day, for example, Azar had a meeting at the White House with presidential chief of staff Mark Meadows on a different matter. He pitched the Operation Warp Speed concept to him for the first time. He got a favorable reaction.

Two days later, on April 15, Azar and I went to the White House to brief the president's counselor and son-in-law, Jared Kushner, on the depleted state of the Strategic National Stockpile. We took the opportunity to pitch the Warp Speed concept too. Jared grasped it immediately and was very enthusiastic about supporting it.

On April 21, Azar contacted Art Levinson, former CEO of

Genentech, to inquire about who might lead this effort and whether he would consider it.

On April 23, we met again with Kushner to discuss the Strategic National Stockpile. Azar laid out his thinking about who could potentially lead the effort and the talent we needed from the private sector. Kushner insisted that Azar, with his experience both at Lilly and in a former administration, lead it himself. This was our approval to launch.

Levinson called back on the April 24. His advice was not to worry about getting a "big brand name" in to run Warp Speed. Rather, we should focus on getting great project management skills. This further reinforced the concept of having ultra-experienced outsiders lead development, distribution, and manufacturing.

Also, on April 24, even though several news outlets were announcing that he was about to be fired, Azar spent the day on the phone, pitching the Warp Speed concept to key administration players. These included Mark Esper (secretary of defense), Chad Wolf (acting DHS secretary), Robert Wilkie (secretary of Veterans Affairs), Kelvin Droegemeier (head of the White House Office of Science and Technology), Sonny Perdue (secretary of agriculture), Dan Brouillet (secretary of energy), Larry Kudlow (head of the National Economic Council), Robert O'Brien (national security advisor to the president), Russ Vought (acting head of the Office of Management and the Budget), and Dr. Deborah Birx. All were enthusiastic. Azar was already laying the foundation for success by aligning those whose support the operation would eventually require.

These were strategic calls, as well as lining up cabinet support. Homeland Security was working on COVID medical countermeasures. Agriculture was involved with vaccine development for animal diseases. Energy had the most advanced computational capabilities within the US government. Azar knew his way around the government from his previous time at HHS.

On May 1, Azar, along with Kushner, visited Secretary Esper at the Pentagon and secured the support of the Army Material Command, led by General Gus Perna, who became a key Warp Speed leader. At this meeting, the two secretaries also agreed on the overall architecture of the operation. The collaboration between Azar and Esper, and their departments, was remarkable and unprecedented. Both secretaries deserve a lot of credit for setting this tone.

On May 13, two days before the Rose Garden kick-off, Azar briefed President Trump in person on Warp Speed. Kushner had already brought the president up to speed. Mr. Trump embraced the plan right away.

I will pause here to underline the scope of the challenge.

I cannot emphasize too strongly that it reached far beyond the science of developing a working vaccine. The science was vital, of course, and Operation Warp Speed's investments eventually supported the work of six companies (Pfizer declined up-front support) working with three vaccine-technology platforms. We remained open initially to the potential of a seventh company, but one never fully materialized.

The preponderance of publicity has gone to the mRNA technology platform. It had been under development for over a decade and was the basis for the two vaccines (Pfizer-BioNTech and Moderna) that reached the public before the end of 2020. But we also invested in the replication-defective live-vector platform (used by J&J/Janssen and AstraZeneca) and the recombinant-subunit-adjuvanted protein platform (used by Sanofi/GSK and Novavax).[14] Merck tried to produce two separate vaccines using two additional platforms: the "replicating viral vector" platform and a platform based on an already-in-use measles vaccine developed at the highly regarded Paris-based Pasteur Institute.[15] Both of Merck's programs failed early testing, and Merck dropped out of the Warp Speed program in early 2021.

But discovery of a vaccine was only the start. In less than six months, Warp Speed had to structure and conduct clinical trials exceeding 100,000 human subjects across well over 100 clinical trial sites.[16]

As well, there was no excess vaccine manufacturing capacity in the United States in January of 2020, so OWS helped to expand, or stood-up, over two dozen facilities focused on bulk vaccine manufacturing, fill-finish capacity, and vaccine vial production.[17] This required flying in special equipment from all over the world, securing raw materials, securing manufacturing sites, training workers for the plants, and establishing quality-control procedures.

The OWS team also enlisted medical supply companies to procure and assemble into kits the more than 1 billion needles and syringes necessary to vaccinate the entire nation.[18]

To do all this, it had to engage, organize, and build a team out of some of the most capable names in American industry: McKesson (to develop warehousing, packaging, and shipping protocols), Palantir to develop a sophisticated information technology-supported distribution system application, FedEx and UPS (to undertake the actual shipping), and Walgreens, CVS, and hundreds of other food and drug retailers, as well as hospitals and clinics to perform the inoculations.

America is the only nation in the world capable of assembling the ingredients of exceptional leadership, private-sector mobilization, ingenuity, and talent in the same place at the same time, and that is why less than one year after the genetic characterization of the COVID-19 virus, it was the only nation distributing millions of doses of multiple safe and effective vaccines to its people.[19] Indeed, despite the media's attempt to criticize the roll-out of vaccine administration, the facts contradict their narrative.

In the early weeks of the roll-out, there were reporting lags in data on how many Americans had been vaccinated on any given day. As well, many experts *overestimated* how many front-line healthcare workers wanted the vaccine. There were differences across jurisdictions regarding who *should* be vaccinated first.

There are always uncertainties in any undertaking this significant. In business, we refer to these as "residual uncertainties," those uncertainties that cannot be effectively assessed no matter how much analysis one conducts. The only resolution to these uncertainties is time. One must let the plan play out, and only then will it be possible to transform uncertainty into certainty.

The key to the success in situations where residual uncertainties are large is rapid learning and adaptation, and this was demonstrated by the federal government and by local leaders across all sixty-four jurisdictions—states, territories, commonwealths, and the District of Columbia. This is why all Americans desiring a vaccine had access to one by the middle of April 2021, scarcely fifteen months after the COVID-19 virus made its debut.[20]

With speed the most critical factor in saving lives, our approach was "design it, try it, fix it, and scale it." This proved the most effective means of getting the maximum number of Americans desiring a vaccine inoculated as quickly as possible.

Also, at every stage we engaged numerous partners—multiple developers, multiple manufacturers, multiple shippers, and multiple inoculators. If one failed (and some did), we had others running on parallel tracks, carrying the baton. Sure, we could have attempted to perfect all aspects of the roll-out before proceeding, but we would have lost months.

2

THE TEAM

Leaders within business, professional sports, government, and politics know that talent and teamwork are often at odds with each other. Too often, the more talented the individuals, the less teamwork seems achievable. Egos, desire for disproportionate recognition, and hubris are often the obstacles to making "one plus one equal three." Operation Warp Speed was totally different, and the difference started at the top.

PRESIDENT DONALD TRUMP: EXECUTIVE SPONSOR

I had only limited working exposure to President Trump before Operation Warp Speed, and this was in support of rebuilding the

Strategic National Stockpile. So I was pleasantly surprised when the man I saw in our meetings proved nothing like the man I read and heard about from the media. He was smart, focused, respectful of our experts, well-briefed, attentive to detail, posed insightful questions, and absolutely understood his role in opening doors and facilitating action. He kept his eye on essentials. His experience as a successful private sector leader turned out to be in complete synchronization with the concepts underpinning the operation.

With everything else that was happening, I would have certainly understood less from him. During the administration's year and a month of COVID, the president faced two impeachment attempts from congressional Democrats. Not to be outdone, his critics in the White House media pool began turning all his COVID media briefings into disruptive heckling sessions. In the summer of 2020, as burning and looting were impacting city after city, state and local officials resisted federal intervention and support. Yet with all this turmoil surrounding him, he never once was anything but focused and encouraging in our OWS meetings with him.

Heritage Foundation scholars Doug Badger and Robert E. Moffit noted in a recent retrospective of the COVID response that "where the historical Washington pattern has been to centralize power and expand regulation, the Trump administration decentralized regulatory power and encouraged private-sector innovation, ranging from small firms to large corporations."[1] They termed Operation Warp Speed, "an aggressive program to remove federal regulatory barriers private companies faced in developing and deploying innovative vaccines."

Yes, it was all that, but it was more.

The plan we presented to the president called for bypassing the normal bureaucratic structures and acquiring management talent and operational capacities from both inside and outside the department and the government. We wanted people and partners who were the best in the nation and the world at what we would ask them to do. Mr. Trump endorsed this wholeheartedly.

In recruiting partner organizations, Trump supported our intention to reach well beyond the pharmaceutical companies that became our ultimate vaccine development picks.

We would also engage twelve specialized pharmaceutical and related supply manufacturers, shippers FedEx, UPS, the distributor McKesson (which specializes in shipping pharmaceuticals), more than seventy supermarket and pharmaceutical chains and their subsidiaries for administering the vaccines, as well as numerous hospital and health clinic organizations, the nation's state and local public health agencies, and many others.[2]

Pfizer initially refused our offer of assistance for vaccine development as it didn't actually discover its vaccine. Taking a vaccine developed by BioNTech, a German biotechnology company, it organized clinical trials and then handled manufacturing and distribution. What Pfizer wanted, and we delivered, was a guaranteed purchase agreement. We met them where they were, so to speak. This was not a one-size-fits-all solution. We also signed a pre-purchase contract with all the other developers, in each case committing the government to buy the company's share in a combined total of 900 million doses. These contracts generally did not depend on the FDA awarding an Emergency Use Authorization (EUA) for the vaccine. Accordingly, the federal government shouldered a significant share of the financial risk involved in development and manufacturing. Trump had a visceral preference for using the private sector. He had just seen its members produce on an emergency basis tens of thousands of ventilators in less than 90 days in response to an anticipated shortage of these devices.

While development and early trials were underway, we engaged the full capacity of twenty-seven vaccine-related manufacturing facilities and made certain they were fully equipped and already manufacturing the new vaccines before the FDA issuing EUAs. In essence, we shouldered the vast majority of the financial risks and ensured that everything was ready to ship immediately upon FDA authorization. We made the government a co-investor and guaranteed buyer, rather than a subsidizer.

We gave the developers (and the manufacturers) the confidence to commit their own funds and talent totally to the goal.

The president approved and encouraged our private sector–heavy approach to operations and our risk-sharing approach to finance. As the weeks progressed, he remained attentive and supportive. In other words, we had an executive sponsor who created an environment for teamwork to thrive, smart risk-taking to flourish, and focus to remain exclusively on the mission, exactly the kind of leadership any high-risk, high-stakes operation needs to prevail.

For me, the most striking endorsement of the president's role came from Moncef Slaoui, our chief scientific officer. During the summer of 2021, in an interview I conducted with him for this book, Moncef made clear that he did not initially support Mr. Trump and was not eager to participate in an initiative that might improve the president's chances for reelection. He understood, however, that, with millions of lives on the line, his expertise was unique and invaluable. He joined the team.

By the time of that interview, Warp Speed was being nearly unanimously hailed as the most effective of the nation's pandemic responses. Looking back, Moncef told me that it had been the best team experience of his career. He gave an important share of the credit to the leadership of President Trump and his willingness to delegate vital tasks to the Warp Speed team leaders. Neither President Trump, nor any of his key advisors at the White House led by Jared Kushner, tried to micromanage the operation from afar. Had they been of a more controlling mindset, it would have led to delays or even failure.

The balance of Operation Warp Speed's senior management team beyond the president totaled eight. Including Secretary Azar and me, only three members came from department-level staff at HHS and one from the department's Food and Drug Administration. Two others joined us from the Defense Department, one a four-star general who was the government's top expert in logistics, the other the military's top expert for developing vaccines to meet bioterror threats. Secretary Esper and Deputy Secretary Norquist deserve a lot of credit for this.

OPERATION WARP SPEED ROLES AND RESPONSIBILITIES

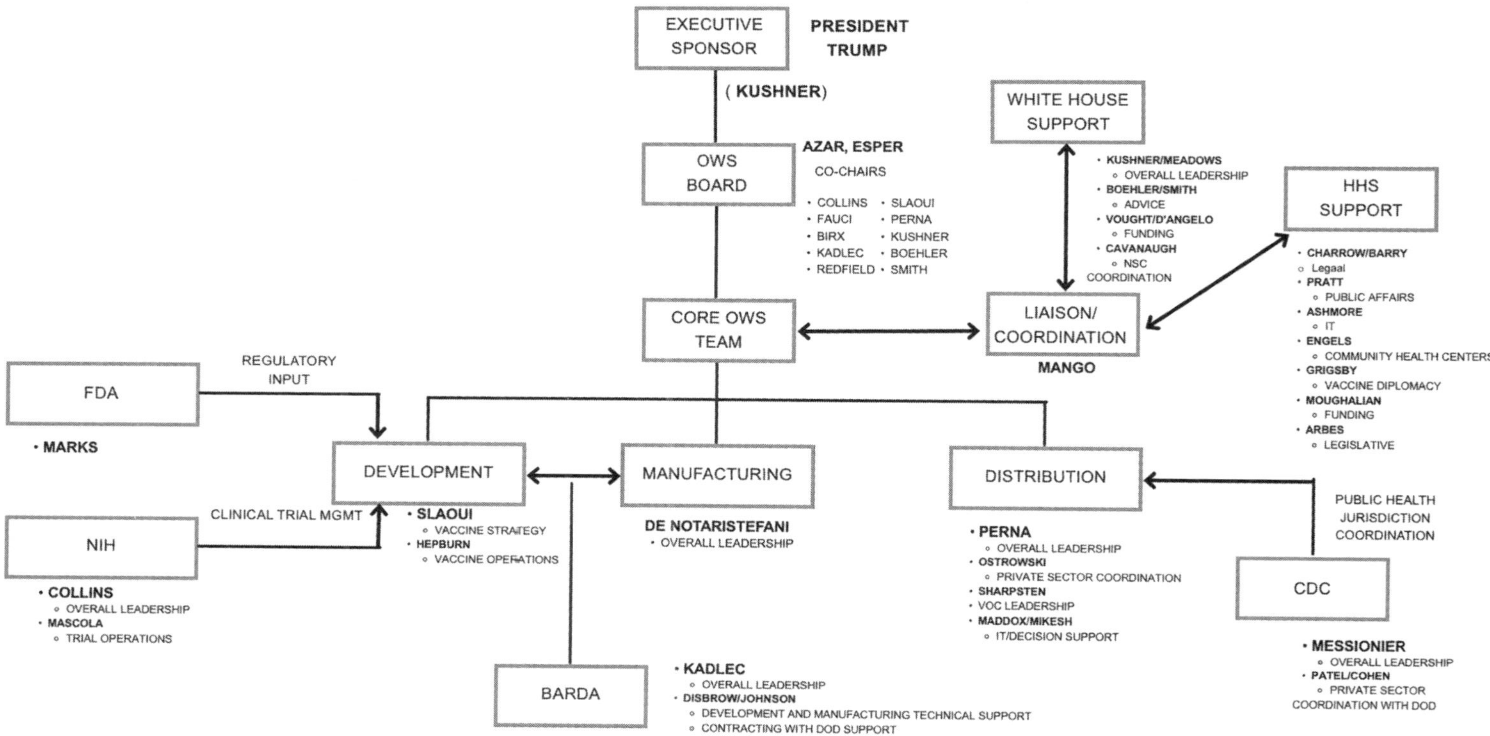

The other two came from industry. Our chief scientific officer was among the global pharmaceutical industry's most experienced and successful vaccine developers. Our lead advisor for manufacturing and supply chain had earned a similar status in acquiring the ingredients for mass-producing vaccines and then the intricate art of making them.

Finally, though not a formal member of the day-to-day management group, Dr. Francis Collins, director of the National Institutes of Health, became a trusted advisor to the team, an invaluable godfather.

HHS SECRETARY ALEX AZAR: THE ARCHITECT

Alex Michael Azar II combined great intellectual capabilities, vast government experience, a deep understanding of the pharmaceutical industry, and a bias for action. Most important, he was resilient.

As 2019 was coming to an end, the new year was not looking good for the secretary. The president was constantly hounding him to take action against rising drug prices. Mr. Trump wanted to push drug prices down and was losing patience with lack of progress in the very difficult and complex area. Then, too, like many other senior Trump administration officials, Azar was under steady attack in the media. Also, a couple of his agency heads were undermining him with hostile leaks to the press. He was characterized as aloof and authoritarian, which could not have been further from the truth. He held others accountable, as any good leader should. Azar himself would agree he was more of a "Patton than an Eisenhower,"[3] but he was fair and consistent. Some simply did not appreciate his style.

Then, six weeks into the pandemic on February 26, 2020, President Trump asked the vice president to lead the national COVID-19 response effort, effectively removing countrywide coordination authority (i.e., working with governors and mayors) from acting White House chief of staff, Mick Mulvaney, who was coordinating the overall response, and from Azar, who was playing a key supporting role. Disappointing at the time, the change led Azar to focus on what became the far more critical initiative of Operation Warp Speed.

Instead of sulking Azar became more resilient. He "stuck to the fight when he was hardest hit."[4.] Nevertheless, for weeks on end, we did not know if it would be his last day in the office. Others in the administration had been unceremoniously dismissed without warning. Would Azar be next?

Alex Azar was born in Johnstown, Pennsylvania, the son of an ophthalmologist who eventually developed a thriving practice in Salisbury, Maryland. His grandfather emigrated from Lebanon almost exactly 100 years before the start of the COVID pandemic. Arriving in the United States in 1920, he went to work for Bethlehem Steel but was injured and had to work as a janitor before eventually owning general stores and bars. When Azar's father was born, his parents initially could not afford to raise him, so they sent him to live with a related Lebanese family in Johnstown. This new guardian's name in Lebanese translated into "Alexander" in English, which is the name the guardian gave Azar's father. When his birth parents had enough money to take him back, they kept the name "Alex," a name his father passed onto his son, the future US cabinet secretary.

Azar's mother's family settled in Windber, Pennsylvania, a small town outside of Johnstown known principally for coal mining. She decided to pursue a career in nursing after high school. She met Azar's father, who had completed medical school at the University of Pittsburgh, while he was completing his internship at the same hospital in Johnstown where she was working.

Attending high school in Salisbury, Maryland, Azar described himself as a "science and math geek," subjects in which he excelled. Similar to the feelings of many families recently immigrated to the United States, a top-quality education for their children meant a lot to Azar's parents. So upon high school graduation, he went off to Dartmouth where he graduated magna cum laude in government and economics. He became politically active there as chairman of the College Republicans, as part of Pete DuPont's presidential campaign in 1988, and as one of the organizers of the presidential debates conducted at Dartmouth during that period.

He had become interested in law after taking a jurisprudence course at Dartmouth and, in the middle of his senior year, he applied to Harvard, Stanford, and Chicago, all of which accepted him. He applied to Yale only on a whim, having just learned from a classmate and friend that Yale had a law school. A few weeks later, he was accepted to Yale and decided this was the place for him.

He continued his conservative activism at Yale as both vice president of the Federalist Society on campus and as one of five members of the *Yale Law Journal* executive committee. During this period, his counterpart at the *Harvard Law Review* was its editor in chief, Barack Obama. The two of them—Azar and Obama—negotiated a deal on a joint business venture between their publications. During his third year in law school, Azar was selected for a Supreme Court clerkship under Antonin Scalia. Later, during the Whitewater investigation, he worked under his mentor Judge Kenneth Starr. Future Supreme Court justice Brett Kavanaugh was a colleague. Joining a private law firm, he worked as the deputy to the head lawyers for the Bush-Cheney team in 2000 and, during that year's extended recount, served on the litigation team in Tallahassee for cases that eventually got resolved in *Bush v Gore*. He then played a role on the George W. Bush transition team, vetting future cabinet officials.

In 2001, still in his early thirties, he was confirmed as general counsel at HHS. At HHS under Secretary Tommy Thompson, Azar dealt with anthrax attacks in 2001 and SARS in 2003. He helped write the Bioterrorism Preparedness Act, passed by Congress in 2003. Later, he helped compose the nation's $7.1 billion pandemic preparedness plan.

Nominated and confirmed as the HHS Deputy Secretary in 2005, he became a major proponent of pharmaceutical and medical device innovation. After leaving the government in 2007, Azar joined Eli Lilly, where he rose to become president of Lilly's US division.

Many, including Azar himself, would say he at times was too passionate, and even defensive about his and his team's perspectives.[5] However, through all these achievements and experiences, he had developed the combination of instinct and confidence, leading him to act decisively. He was precisely the type of leader we needed two months into the most catastrophic pandemic in 100 years.

DR. ROBERT KADLEC: THE COORDINATOR

As the pandemic emerged in early 2020, Dr. Robert Kadlec was serving as the assistant secretary for Preparedness and Response (ASPR), the agency within the Department of Health and Human Services most closely linked to, and responsible for, pandemic response. Kadlec's responsibilities included overseeing the Biomedical Advanced Research and Development Authority (BARDA), which was the organization responsible for the development and procurement of medical countermeasures to combat counterterrorism. These countermeasures included chemical, biological, radiological, and nuclear (CBRN) threats. Established in 2006, BARDA was created by the Pandemic and All-Hazards Preparedness Act (PAHPA). BARDA also managed Project BioShield, which funds the research, development, and stockpiling of vaccines and therapeutics to be used during public health emergencies.

Bob Kadlec was born in Bayside Queens, New York, the son of Czech immigrants. His father was the son of a mayor in Czechoslovakia, whom the Nazis imprisoned after they occupied his homeland. His mother was born in the US to Czech parents who emigrated back to Czechoslovakia during the Great Depression. During the war, Kadlec's future father and mother both wound up in the same forced labor camp, his mother sewing undergarments for German soldiers on the Eastern Front and his father packing and shipping those garments. After the war, his mother, as a US citizen, was permitted to come back to the US, but his father was not. Determined to get back to his future wife, his father made his way across the armed frontier that was the Iron Curtain into Austria and ultimately to the United States.[6] This heritage explains much about a guy who always finds it easier to "beg for forgiveness than to ask permission." Thank goodness we had him as one of the leaders on Operation Warp Speed.

From a young age, Kadlec wanted to be an Air Force flight surgeon.

He entered the United States Air Force Academy after high school graduation in 1975. Bob's uncle had been imprisoned with US Army Air Force pilots in a German prisoner of war camp during World War II, making the family partial to the Air Force.

After graduation, he attended the Uniformed Services University where he earned his medical degree. During more than twenty years in the Air Force, he was assigned to a wide range of bases and units, including the Joint Special Operations Command, the Pentagon, and the Central Intelligence Agency's counterterrorism and counter-proliferation units. He engaged in several covert operations and was embedded into the United Nations team inspecting Iraq for weapons of mass destruction. He served in the George W. Bush White House as both the director of Biodefense on the Homeland Security Council and as a special assistant to the president for biodefense policy.

He also served as Senator Richard Burr's staff director on the Bioterrorism and Public Health Subcommittee. While with the Senate, he was instrumental in the writing and eventual passage of the Pandemic and All Hazards Preparedness Act (PAHPA) of 2006. This act created the role and office of ASPR, overseeing BARDA, both of which Kadlec was leading when the COVID-19 pandemic broke out in early 2020.[7]

With all this time in special operations and on Capitol Hill, and with an extensive personal network that included many former covert operators, needless to say, Kadlec knew how to get things done. Over time, we learned to *not even ask* how he did it. It reminded me of a sergeant in my unit at the 82nd Airborne Division in the early 1980s, who used to tell me, "Sir, if you ask me no questions, I'll tell you no lies." We were in the middle of a pandemic, and we needed resourceful leaders, such as Bob Kadlec, to simply make things happen. With results like his, why pose questions?

Within twenty-four hours of the $450 million Johnson & Johnson investment discovery, Secretary Azar was moving to line up more leaders, such as Bob Kadlec. He knew we did not have the talent inside of HHS beyond Kadlec to pull off what Operation Warp Speed would require—talent with a deep understanding of the contemporary state of vaccine development, manufacturing, and the logistics of getting hundreds of millions of doses to the entire nation in record time.

We quickly established a committee to interview prospective candidates for these roles and invited Dr. Fauci, Jared Kushner, Dr. Birx, members of the DoD, and Adam Boehler to join. Before this, on April 13, Azar picked up the phone and called Jim Greenwood, a former Pennsylvania congressman who at the time was the head of the Biological Innovation Organization (BIO), a trade group representing biologics manufacturers. He had two simple questions for Greenwood: Who is the most successful vaccine developer in the world today, and who is the best manufacturing expert? Greenwood called back within forty-eight hours with two names: Dr. Moncef Slaoui and Carlo de Notaristefani, respectively.

DR. MONCEF SLAOUI: THE VACCINE WIZARD

Moncef Slaoui became our chief scientific officer. One of the world's most successful vaccine developers, during a thirty-year career at GlaxoSmithKline (GSK), he had brought fourteen successful vaccines to market. He understood more than anyone on earth both the biological uncertainties associated with vaccine development and manufacturing, and the keys to ushering a safe and effective vaccine through the rigorous clinical trial and regulatory processes.

Moncef was born and raised in Casablanca, Morocco, the son of an entrepreneur who actively fought against French colonization before Morocco's independence in 1955. Neither of his parents had earned a college degree, yet they insisted that Moncef and his three siblings obtain one. Accordingly, all four children earned either PhDs or medical degrees. Before he was born, Moncef's parents had lost a daughter to whooping cough. Like so many households outside of Western Europe and the United States, the family became acutely aware of contagious disease and the unseen threats to good health.

Moncef showed an affinity for biology at an early age and was eager to attend medical school. In 1976, he went to the Belgian Embassy in Casablanca, seeking admission to the University of Brussels Medical School. He was informed that the medical school slots were already filled but was invited to go to Brussels and sit in on biology classes.

In Brussels, he became active in a group called Moving Forward, which opposed the government in Morocco. He became president of the group. After two years in Belgium, Moncef received word that his mother was gravely ill. He rushed home. Local authorities discovered that the young agitator had returned. He was almost arrested. When explaining to his father that his activism was a means by which he could bring positive change to the world, his father replied: "If you want to change the world, you must stay alive."

Upon returning to Brussels and heeding his father's advice, Moncef stopped agitating and doubled down on studying. He focused on immunology and, under an inspirational professor, earned his PhD. Soon he met a very bright young woman who was working in an adjacent laboratory. They married, and in 1983 went to Harvard for postdoctoral studies. When GlaxoSmithKline's (GSK) Vaccine Division back in Brussels hired her, he returned to the University of Brussels as an assistant professor. Before long, GSK was asking him for advice on vaccines. He joined the company in 1988.

Remembering his sister's death from whooping cough, he became increasingly focused on developing new and effective vaccines, maybe even achieving the global impact he had professed to his father. He returned to the States in 2003 with the ambition of leading all research and development for GSK, a role he assumed in 2006. He retired from GSK in 2017.[8]

Moncef's demeanor is that of a European gentleman. Well-mannered, respectful, considerate, and generally taciturn, he rarely asserts a perspective early in a discussion or unprompted. He is an excellent listener and actively seeks the input of others. When solicited, however, his perspectives are always well-thought-out, logical, penetrating in terms of their insight, and highly ethical.

When initially contacted about the role to become chief scientific officer of what could be another Manhattan Project, Moncef was frustrated. He was not a supporter of Republican causes and did not want the president reelected, but he knew this would ultimately be about saving lives. Within a week of being called by BIO's Jim Greenwood and then by Bob Kadlec, Moncef was in DC for a round of interviews.[9]

Among the candidates for Warp Speed's chief scientific advisor, Moncef stood out. He exuded a quiet confidence about the mission itself. He was the only candidate who genuinely believed we could have one or more safe and effective vaccines before year's end. He was also the only one with deep ties to the commercial vaccine development community.

We understood OWS would only be successful as a public-private partnership, and Moncef had earned the respect and trust of the commercial vaccine development community. The most important characteristic revealed during the interview process, however, came in the form of an answer to the question about how he formed teams and motivated others. His response was precisely the one we wanted: "I delegate many tasks, take accountability for failure, and give all the credit for success to others."

CARLO DE NOTARISTEFANI: THE MEDICINE MANUFACTURING MARVEL

Carlo de Notaristefani was our lead advisor, Manufacturing and Supply Chain. Born in southern Italy near Naples, the first of three children in a well-established family, he had spent his career in pharmaceutical manufacturing, operations, and supply-chain management.

His father was a chemical engineer, his mother a university professor of French literature. As an undergraduate, he believed he would take over his father's business, so he studied chemical engineering. The oil shocks of the 1970s eventually drove his father's business into bankruptcy, but Carlo persisted with his focus on chemical engineering, eventually earning a doctorate from the University of Naples.

Italy still had mandatory military service, so Carlo spent eighteen months in the Italian army after graduation. Atypical for most draftees, Carlo's time in uniform was spent on a vital mission: rebuilding an Italian community suffering from the after-effects of a recent earthquake. During this assignment, he observed something that stuck with him throughout his career. As opposed to the boredom and indifference that he knew most Italian draftees felt during their service, Carlo and his team felt a keen sense of mission. He had no trouble motivating his soldiers to work fourteen to sixteen hours per day, seven days a week without complaint, as they helped people of the town and region recover. During an interview, he commented that he observed this same keen sense of mission among the Warp Speed team members.

After completing military service, he began the journey of building the impressive profile of a globally experienced executive. He spent many years among several pharmaceutical companies, which changed hands through mergers, and he relocated five times between Europe and the US before being named president of technical operations and global support functions at Bristol-Myers Squibb in 2004. He became president and chief executive officer of Israeli-based Teva Pharmaceutical Industry's global operations in 2012. He retired from Teva in 2019, shortly before the pandemic broke out.

When Bob Kadlec contacted him about involvement in a Manhattan-like project for a COVID vaccine, Carlo jumped at the opportunity. COVID had put an end to planned retirement travel, and he admitted he "was going crazy sitting at home during the shutdown."[10] Also, Carlo loved sailing. His retirement plan was to do a lot of it. COVID forced scrapping that, too. In other words, his time was entirely his own, and he was eager to get in on the world's biggest and most urgent vaccine action.

Carlo was meticulous about quality throughout his tenure on OWS and personified the aphorism "an ounce of prevention is worth a pound of cure," though at times some members of the OWS team thought he measured prevention by the pound, or ton. But Carlo knew well that getting past the FDA's high standards required demonstrating stable, repeatable manufacturing operations. Dr. Slaoui commented on many occasions that developing vaccines would be the easy part. The much more uncertain part would be manufacturing them with quality at scale.

Under Carlo's guidance and leadership, the US went from having zero excess vaccine manufacturing capacity in the spring of 2020 to producing hundreds of millions of safe and effective vaccines a year later. It was a remarkable achievement that few outside of the endlessly intricate, exacting world of pharmaceutical manufacturing can fully appreciate.

GENERAL GUSTAVE PERNA: THE LOGISTICS GENIUS

General Gustave (Gus) Perna, could not have come from a more different background than Moncef Slaoui or Carlo de Notaristefani. Yet during a Pentagon meeting with Secretary Mark Esper and General Mark Milley, Azar posed a simple question: who is the best logistics leader in the Defense Department? The response was immediate: General Gustave Perna.

Gus Perna grew up in New Jersey in an ethnically Italian family and often refers with great admiration to his mother, whose advice he still receives whether he seeks it or not. With an incisive intellect and wry sense of humor, when someone raised an issue irrelevant to addressing the challenge at hand, he often responded, "I am only mildly interested in the point you just made; here's what we need to focus on."

He claims he was an average student who "worked hard," but those who know him understand this form self-deprecation is only an effective means of disarming those who would otherwise be intimidated by the four stars on each of his shoulders. Of the hundreds of thousands of active-duty personnel and of the tens of thousands of officers the United States Army had when we interviewed him, there were only fourteen four-star generals[11.] No one achieves four stars in today's Army by being average at anything.

Perna entered the Army via the Valley Forge Military Academy and College, where he was a distinguished graduate. He rose through the ranks of the Army Material Command, the branch of the service responsible for supplying our soldiers with food, ammunition, weapons, uniforms, and anything else they need to be successful on the battlefield. By 2020, after nearly two decades of supporting continuous combat operations in the Middle East following the 9/11terrorist attacks, the Army Material Command was a well-developed, well-led, experienced, and resourceful team unparalleled anywhere in the world. More than anything else, Perna understood the key to success in the extraordinarily complex world of military logistics: make every task as simple as possible.

Decades of experience had taught him the vital difference between the *planning* of logistics and the *physics* of logistics. At some point, he knew that our team's task would come down to delivering hundreds of millions of vaccines, along with the requisite needles, syringes, swabs, and masks necessary to administer the vaccine to the right places, at the right times, and in the right quantities under the right stringent transport and storage conditions.

Despite their polar opposite backgrounds, Slaoui, the refined, sophisticated, European executive strategist from the private sector and Perna, the "can do, take no prisoners" logistics expert from New Jersey with more than thirty years in the US military, formed a legendary partnership borne out of mutual respect and admiration.

Several months into their relationship, Moncef very cleverly adopted some of the military vernacular, such as referring to his commitment to maintaining the "battle rhythm" and finishing his statements by using the word *over*. It was a subtle way of expressing his respect for all the military was bringing to the approach and success of the mission. More important, it was an expression of solidarity and joint commitment to the singular objective on which both leaders were focused: *save American lives.*

DR. PETER MARKS: EARLY SCREENER, LATER REVIEWER

In early 2020, Dr. Peter Marks was the director of the FDA's Center for Biologics Evaluation and Research, otherwise known as "CBER," at the US Food and Drug Administration (FDA). CBER is the organization within the US government responsible for evaluating the safety and effectiveness of drugs based on products known as "biologics."

For the average American, this generally means those drugs injected into the body as shots, rather than swallowed as pills. Peter is the epitome of a senior federal government career official: extremely knowledgeable in his field, deadly serious, emotionally committed to the mission of his agency, and a tireless worker.

He was born in Brooklyn, New York, and had had a challenging childhood. At an early age, his parents divorced. He lived with his mother in New Jersey. When he was ten, she died in a private airplane crash, and he returned to New York City to live with his father. His interest in medicine began in high school. He loved science and math.

After high school graduation, he ultimately ended up staying in New York to attend Columbia University as an undergraduate. He played the viola in the orchestra, where he met another young musician, now his wife.

While at Columbia, Peter worked at St Luke's Hospital in the clinical laboratory and as a phlebotomist. Working with great doctors sparked his interest in going to medical school. He earned his medical degree and PhD at New York University's School of Medicine and then completed a residency at Brigham and Women's hospital in Boston, where he eventually specialized in hematology/oncology.

He joined the staff there but left for private industry after about five years, joining a Cambridge, Massachusetts-based biotechnology company, Genzyme (now known as SanofiGenzyme), then moving on to Novartis. Understanding how the private pharmaceutical industry worked was a key contributor to Peter's success later in his career as the head of the FDA's CBER.

He quickly tired of private industry and returned to academic medicine at Yale, where he ran the adult leukemia and clinical cancer services. He joined the FDA as the deputy director of CBER in 2012 and became its director in 2016.[12]

In February, just weeks after learning of COVID-19, it was clear to him and to his colleagues that a pandemic would be inevitable. By March, he and his team were scanning the globe and the literature, attempting to identify potentially promising COVID-19 vaccine developments.

One of his early instincts however was to advance the possible use of a therapeutic known as convalescent plasma, a technique whereby those who had recently recovered from a disease donate antibody-rich plasma to those recently infected. This technique had been used for about a century and occasionally proved effective.

As we entered into March, several companies began talking about vaccine development but, generally, with anticipated time frames extending into 2022. This stimulated Peter to think about how the FDA, and CBER in particular, could accelerate the process by which it evaluated the safety and efficacy of vaccines.

Shortly thereafter, he contacted Bob Kadlec, who was overseeing BARDA, to see if Bob had ideas regarding how vaccine manufacturing could be accelerated as well.[13] The three of us, along with secretary Azar, met by phone on April 10, shortly after Azar began setting up the entire Operation Warp Speed enterprise. By that time, according to Peter, somewhere between 90–100 vaccine candidates were under development.[14]

During the call, we discussed the importance of developing a scoring system to flag the most promising candidates. For many reasons described later, the federal government would not be supporting 100 vaccine candidates but was quite eager to accelerate a much smaller number of the most promising ones. Out of this exercise, Marks and Kadlec identified fourteen vaccines whose companies possessed the scientific and logistical capacity to develop, evaluate, manufacture, and distribute tens of millions of vaccines in a reasonable time frame. It was from this list of fourteen that Moncef Slaoui eventually selected the slate of six vaccine candidates to back.

Based on the initiative Dr. Marks had already taken and his deep knowledge of the global pharmaceutical biologics sector, Secretary Azar and we were eager to have him play a key leadership role in the vaccine initiative. Indeed, it was Peter Marks who actually coined the term "Operation Warp Speed," superseding Azar's initial moniker, "Manhattan Project II."

Assuming a role within Operation Warp Speed would have required

Dr. Marks to recuse himself temporarily from his leadership role at CBER, which he was initially willing to do. So we asked him to put together a brief perspective in PowerPoint format and be prepared to share it with the senior team at HHS, and eventually with those at the White House. He did so rapidly and enthusiastically, but by late April, two events had materially changed his desire to leave CBER and to help lead Warp Speed's vaccine development. The first was a critical meeting in the White House Situation Room convened by Dr. Deborah Birx in the afternoon of April 29.

Dr. Birx is one of the world's most renowned epidemiologists. Having been appointed President Obama's Global AIDS Coordinator to the "President's Emergency Plan for AIDS Relief," or PEPFAR, in 2014, she acquired both a wealth of experience in controlling the spread of HIV/AIDS in Sub-Saharan Africa, and the title of ambassador.[15, 16]

She grew up in Lancaster, Pennsylvania, the daughter of well-educated parents and the sibling of scientifically oriented brothers. Scientifically precocious herself and competitive at an early age, she earned several accolades while in high school, completed her undergraduate collegiate studies in two years, and then attended medical school at Penn-State Hershey. As an active-duty Army officer in the 80s and 90s, Dr. Birx spent a good deal of her time at the Walter Reed Army Medical Center and the National Institutes of Health under the guidance and mentorship of Drs. Anthony Fauci and Robert Redfield, both of whom eventually co-led, along with Dr. Birx, various aspects of the COVID-19 pandemic response for the US government. She also spent time as a career official at CDC until appointed "Ambassador-at-Large" by President Obama.

In late February 2020, Vice President Mike Pence appointed Dr. Birx to the White House Coronavirus Task Force as its "response coordinator."[17] In a matter of weeks, her influence and leadership were pervasive. Knowing how antiquated the CDC's data acquisition and management systems were, she got to work on creating altogether new ones with the help of the data and analytics firm Palantir. Clearly, she understood that knowledge and data meant power, and she was intent on wielding it. As the saying goes, "In the land of the blind, the cyclops is king." Deb Birx was going to have privileged access to data, and thereby become "the king," exercising control over the federal government's entire response. Within a matter of weeks, not a single decision, publication, press release, or investment in such things as laboratory testing capacity was cleared without her approval. For all of Deborah Birx's towering strengths, however, she quickly and consistently exhibited two critical weaknesses.

First, she was limited by what she knew. In nearly every conversation, she would allude to what she had done successfully to fight HIV/AIDS in Africa. This was the playbook with which she was familiar, and she was determined to replicate it. The only problems with this were that COVID-19 was not HIV/AIDS, and the United States was not Africa.

Second, she consistently brought more heat than light to group settings and did so in ways that berated and belittled others. All of this was a shame, as Dr. Birx had much to offer. She could often be right from a content perspective but too destructive from a style perspective. This was all the more perplexing as she was very engaging and a careful listener in one-on-one interactions.

One of the early demonstrations of this destructive style came in late April when Peter Marks, the president's chief of staff Mark Meadows, and a group of us met with her in the White House Situation Room. As the COVID-19 response coordinator, Dr. Birx had appropriately been requesting an update on where HHS stood with the development of "medical countermeasures," the government's term for vaccines, diagnostics, and therapeutics. Though just days into his unofficial role as the head of vaccines for the not-yet-named Operation Warp Speed initiative, and while still deeply involved in his day job of leading CBER, Dr. Marks had agreed at my request to be the Warp Speed team's lead presenter.

There are no niceties at the start of a Dr. Birx-led meeting. It is always all business. In this case, this rigid, no-niceties, put-up-the-slides approach gave Marks no opportunity to introduce himself or explain his formal role in CBER, or that he had been asked just days before to assemble a perspective on where we stood with vaccine development.

The meeting started with Meadows inquiring about the lack of vaccine manufacturing capacity and why we hadn't already stood up more of it. Azar calmly described that vaccine manufacturing differed greatly from making widgets, or even greatly from making the ventilators, whose manufacturing capacity the president had recently expanded.

Then Dr. Birx jumped in, assaulting Marks with questions, not waiting for his responses, and inquiring why *he* had not more thoroughly evaluated the potential vaccine candidates. She was furious that Marks hadn't been focusing on the protein sub-unit vaccines she was so accustomed to using in Africa. She asserted that mRNA vaccines for COVID would never be successful and implied we were investing in them as a means of compensating for their failed cancer programs. She was adamant about Genentech's Chinese Hamster Ovaries (CHO) production capabilities and capacity as the answer to our vaccine challenge. Being the gentleman he was, Peter calmly tried several times to explain that he was in the process of conducting just such an evaluation, but Dr. Birx would hear none of it. She was livid. Azar and I followed Birx to her office after this session and explained to her that these were the early steps, not the conclusion, of what would become Warp Speed. She settled down and was supportive.

Chief Meadows was more sympathetic. He pressed Peter on several fronts, not as a means of berating him but rather as a means of better understanding the current situation. Indeed, a couple of days after this session, Meadows bumped into Dr. Marks at the White House and apologized for the prior meeting's "fireworks."[18] The meeting did not last long. It was clear to others in the room that this was not the type of collaborative interaction one typically observes among colleagues in the medical profession. As Dr. Fauci and Secretary Azar were leaving the meeting, Fauci put his arm around Azar and commented, "Don't worry, Alex, the mRNA vaccines are going to work."[19]

At about the same time this meeting took place, we were finishing our interviews for appointing a chief scientific advisor to our team. It had become clear that Dr. Moncef Slaoui was going to fill this role. Peter knew of Dr. Slaoui and his remarkable success in vaccine development.

The combination of the demoralizing meeting with Dr. Birx and the fact that we were bringing Dr. Slaoui on board led Peter to realize that his most valuable role in Warp Speed would be to insure CBER was organized and led in such a way that, without compromising any quality standards, it could rapidly evaluate what would soon be a slate of vaccine candidates for emergency use authorization (EUA). Out of his tremendous respect for Dr. Marks, Azar lobbied him to stay with the OWS, but Peter left the team to concentrate on the regulatory task.

DR. MATT HEPBURN: THE DEVELOPMENT COORDINATOR

When Peter Marks decided to relinquish the role as our vaccines head and return to the FDA, Dr. Matt Hepburn took his place.[20] Like Peter, Matt's job was overseeing our investment in six COVID vaccine developers and facilitating the partnerships necessary for them to succeed.

Matt came from a family steeped in the value of selfless service. His grandfather, a veteran of World War I, died when Matt's dad was very young with the result that the boy developed a strong sense of responsibility at a very early age. His father eventually attended Villanova University on a Navy ROTC scholarship, served on active duty as a nuclear engineer, and then served as a reservist for thirty years, retiring as a captain. His mother also exemplified a life of service as a nurse. By the time Hepburn reached high school, it had become clear to him that he was headed to the military.

He earned an Army ROTC scholarship to Duke where he graduated in 1992 and stayed on to receive his medical degree in 1996. He specialized in internal medicine but developed a keen interest in infectious diseases.

Receiving a fellowship to study infectious diseases, Hepburn spent time in Asia and Latin America, studying malaria and other tropical illnesses. With the post-9/11 anthrax attacks, he realized for the first time that we needed not only to fight Mother Nature when it came to bacterial and viral afflictions but bad actors as well.

When the government committed to developing vaccines against anthrax and other dangerous agents, Hepburn went to Fort Detrick, Maryland, the Army's highly secure location for such programs. As part of this effort, he was an exchange officer in the United Kingdom for a couple of years. From there, he spent the next few years on a Department of Defense program aimed at partnering with the republics of the former Soviet Union in developing their public health systems. Research centers in these countries had significant expertise in infectious diseases. During the Soviet period, they had been devoted to biological warfare. Hepburn's program facilitated their transition to public health purposes. Working with these scientists inspired him to focus his career on combatting infectious diseases.

When the H1N1 outbreak hit in 2009, he was just returning from a tour in Iraq. He was asked to join the National Security Council to codify H1N1 "lessons learned," a job that led to his becoming more familiar with the Department of Health and Human Services, the CDC, and further expanding his government network of like-minded professionals. He then moved on to the Defense Advanced Research Projects Agency (DARPA) as part of its Rapid Response unit, where he learned about biologics manufacturing.

In early 2020, he emerged as the DoD's principal specialist on vaccines and joined General Perna's OWS team in that role. He felt like he had been preparing his entire professional career for this moment.

DR. FRANCIS COLLINS: THE GODFATHER

In 2009, President Obama picked Dr. Francis Collins to lead the National Institutes of Health. President Trump reappointed him. From the start, he was a highly trusted partner and advisor to all of us in the Operation Warp Speed team, our "godfather."

Dr. Collins was born and reared on a small farm in Virginia's Shenandoah Valley and was homeschooled until the sixth grade.

Unusual for that period, the homeschooling was a function of parents both deeply committed to education and having little confidence in the public school system.

His parents had met at Yale University in 1931, where they were both enrolled in post-graduate work, so they clearly understood the difference between a good and poor education. Collins became interested in science during high school but focused principally on chemistry rather than biology.

After graduating from high school at age sixteen, he attended the University of Virginia where he graduated with a bachelor's degree in chemistry. He went on to earn a PhD in physical chemistry at Yale, focusing on what he admits was, at the time, a relative obscure aspect of the field, quantum mechanics. While working toward the doctorate, he became much more interested in biology and was eventually offered a scholarship to study medicine at the University of North Carolina School of Medicine. After earning a medical degree, he returned to Yale to conduct genetics research. In 1984, he accepted a faculty position at the University of Michigan.[21]

It was at Michigan where he first committed to use what he had learned in genetics to tackle a complex and difficult medical challenge: characterize the genetic cause of cystic fibrosis, a disease whose victims, at that time, rarely made it past their teen years. It was about this time that he also learned the value of collaboration over competition to achieve common goals, a lesson that served him well during Operation Warp Speed. He joined forces with a Canadian researcher at the Hospital for Sick Children in Toronto in the fight to characterize cystic fibrosis. Five years later, in 1989, they had successfully identified the three omitted genetic letters leading to cystic fibrosis out of 3 billion in the human genome.

In 1993, he received a call from Dr. Bernadine Healy, at the time the director of the NIH. Jim Watson, who had been leading the Human Genome Project there had recently been dismissed, and Dr. Healy wanted Collins to replace him. So, in April of 1993, Collins joined the National Institutes of Health (NIH) as the director of its Center for

Human Genome Research. Again, Dr. Collins turned to collaboration as the means of reaching the goal Watson had set out: characterize the entire human genome by 2005. He set about organizing and coordinating twenty different laboratories in six different countries, ultimately comprising approximately 2,400 scientists.

In 1998, Craig Venter had broken out of the joint effort to start Celera, and the race to characterize the genome took on a competitive undertone. Once more, Collins thought collaboration would be better than competition. In 2000, he and Venter were honored at a White House ceremony, celebrating their joint achievements. He eventually completed the full characterization of the human genome in 2003, two years early and $400 million under budget.[22] This made him a darling of the Capitol Hill. For all these spectacular accomplishments, he was awarded the Presidential Medal of Freedom in 2007.[23]

He stayed at the NIH building on his research until 2008, when he resigned to contemplate his next career steps. A year later, he was asked to join the Obama transition team tasked with staffing the NIH and was eventually asked by the team to fill the director's role.

Somewhat atypical for such an accomplished scientist, Dr. Collins is a motorcycle enthusiast. When I asked him how he became interested in motorcycles, he said he had little or no money as an undergraduate at the University of Virginia, so he bought a motorbike to get around. He is also a musician, a love and talent he picked up from his father, a well-known folk music collector who provided advice at their home to the likes of Bob Dylan when Francis was a child.[24]

Under Secretary Azar, Dr. Collins would hold terrific weekly scientific tutorials for us. He could take very complex scientific topics and break them down such that even lay persons like Azar and me could understand them. It became the highlight of our week before COVID appeared. Azar had known and worked with Dr. Collins for over two decades. He viewed Dr. Collins as his closest operating division head colleague, both personally and professionally, even though Dr. Collins was originally an Obama appointee.

TRANSFORMING TALENT INTO A TEAM

It was a compelling and pressing mission that brought this team together. Everyone understood what was at stake. By the late spring of 2020, it was clear to all of us that nothing but safe and effective vaccines would save the United States from a catastrophic outcome in terms of both human and economic destruction.

The pivotal role in team building, however, played out at the next level of the Operation Warp Speed enterprise, and this is where General Perna and Dr. Slaoui resided. As noted earlier, these two leaders came from completely different backgrounds: Moncef from Morocco, Gus from New Jersey; Moncef from the private sector, Gus from the public sector. Both had risen to the tops of their respective professions, but one through scientific prowess and one through logistical acumen.

Matt Hepburn, who observed Moncef and Gus daily, described why he believed these two got along so well and had so much mutual respect. Over their careers, Hepburn noted, the two had developed a strikingly similar set of executive leadership principles: clarity of communications, a low tolerance for hidden agendas, a deep sense of commitment to and respect for those serving underneath them, fact-based decision-making, and "selfless-servant" mindsets as leaders[25].

This last point is perhaps the most important. Neither of these leaders has big egos. They were thrust into a global spotlight on May 15, 2020, in the Rose Garden of the White House, yet that afternoon, they were back in the HHS Humphrey Building toiling away at the challenges of the mission. Indeed, for several months, they specifically requested that we *not* put them before the media, despite scores of requests. They were too busy working on behalf of their core task. This selfless-servant mindset stood in stark contrast to many members of the White House Task Force. You did not want to find yourself between some of these task force members and a camera for fear of being stampeded.

There were other selfless, collaborative leaders that formed the bulwark of the Operation Warp Speed leadership team: Dr. Francis

Collins from the NIH, who, as noted earlier, made a successful career out of collaboration; Bob Kadlec, who learned about teamwork as a cadet at the United States Air Force Academy; and the other senior leaders under General Perna's command, such as Lieutenant General (ret.) Paul Ostrowski and Major General Chris Sharpsten. This spirit of collaboration and commitment permeated down through the ranks of Operation Warp Speed. No one could ever find daylight between Perna and Slaoui on key issues, and therefore, no one attempted to lobby either of them at the expense of the other.

3

THE LAUNCH

ROSE GARDEN KICKOFF—MAY 15, 2020

May 15 was an unusually hot spring day in Washington, DC. We had assembled the core leadership team of Secretary Azar, Slaoui, de Notaristefani, Collins, and Perna at the White House. Additionally, Janet Woodcock from the FDA, who had stepped up to lead therapeutics development within OWS, Peter Marks who was at the time still leading vaccine development, and Stephen Hahn, commissioner of the FDA, Dr. Fauci, Dr. Birx, and Dr. Collins were all present with us in the Rose Garden for the ceremony with President Trump to officially launch Operation Warp Speed.

Scarcely six weeks from the conception of OWS, we had identified, interviewed, recruited, and brought on-board the leaders who would make such a difference. We also crystallized the strategy of identifying the most promising vaccine candidates and investing on an at-risk basis in manufacturing millions of doses *before* those companies seeking and receiving FDA authorization. This was the only way we had the chance of vaccinating any American desiring a vaccine before the middle of 2021. Making the right decisions could not have been more important, and that required a highly knowledgeable, experienced team.

The seats in the Rose Garden were set quite far apart out of respect for COVID, the grass was wet, and the ground was soft. So when one sat down, the folding chair sank a couple of inches into the ground. When the sun came out, the moisture from the grass transformed into a fine steamy mist. Everyone was sweating.

JARED KUSHNER AND THE PUBLIC ROLLOUT

Jared was our all-important link to the White House and especially to the president.

I had worked closely with him earlier in the year on rebuilding HHS's Strategic National Stockpile for pandemic emergencies, the reserves that the prior administration had depleted and never replenished. He was instrumental in helping us mobilize American industry to manufacture tens of thousands of ventilators in approximately ninety days' time. There was no question about his ability to make things happen.

Jared had already become involved with Operation Warp Speed, interviewing Moncef for his job on our team and liking him for the same reasons the rest of us did. The Rose Garden kickoff was Jared's next big contribution to the Warp Speed effort. He knew well the signal this would send to the rest of the White House, the balance of the federal government, and to the nation.

Specifically, it meant that the president cared about this issue. The impact of this cannot be overstated. From that point on, Operation Warp Speed had legitimacy, and this meant the other elements of the federal government lined up behind it. Jared was also very politically astute. He understood right away how important it would be for the president to be clearly positioned as the executive sponsor of Operation Warp Speed, an effort so crucial to extinguishing the impact of the virus in the United States.

After a short wait, Mr. Trump, along with Moncef, General Perna, Secretary Azar, Secretary Esper, Dr. Birx, Dr. Collins, and Dr. Fauci entered the Rose Garden from inside the White House. The president was in a buoyant mood as he was interrupted several times by the loud horns of scores of eighteen-wheel tractor trailers parked a couple hundred yards away on Constitution Avenue. Thousands of truckers had descended on DC that week to rally in support of him.

When I later asked Moncef about the Rose Garden event, he said he had been notified only early that morning that the president might ask him to say a few words. As he stepped to the microphone, he decided that he needed to subordinate his "discomfort with certainty" as a scientist and, instead, play the role of a confident leader.[1]

Moncef announced to the entire world we would have at least one safe and effective vaccine before year's end. He described this afterward as feeling like he "was jumping off a cliff without a parachute." When asked about meeting the president for the first time that day, he was surprised at how "approachable and normal" he was.[2]

General Perna was always appropriately skeptical about being thrust into what could be perceived as political events. As a high-ranking officer in the Army, his role was to support his commander-in-chief but never to appear political. The president, on the other hand, appeared to appreciate having a general in uniform at the podium. Nonetheless, after brief remarks by the president, Secretary Azar, and Dr. Slaoui, General Perna gracefully introduced himself and explained his role. Secretary Esper was also present and spoke at this event. He was forceful in committing the Department of Defense to accomplishing this mission. Mark Esper was a strong and reliable partner in the OWS enterprise. We could not have been successful without his, and the Department of Defense's, unconditional support.

Mr. Trump then answered some questions from the media, and we were done. Operation Warp Speed had completed its official kickoff, and now the world knew the key players and their ambitious objectives. Moncef commented afterward that he was relieved that he had made the commitment publicly to having at least one safe and effective vaccine by year's end. In his mind, it eliminated any uncertainty about that for which we were striving. He found this liberating.[3]

PICKING VACCINE CANDIDATES

In the early spring of 2020, there were already close to 100 COVID-19 vaccines in advanced research or under early development.[4] As discussed earlier, Peter Marks, head of the Center for Biologics Evaluation and Research (CBER) within the FDA, had already begun screening these vaccines and had narrowed the field down to the fourteen most promising ones.

The role of evaluating vaccine candidates began to transition to Moncef Slaoui and Matt Hepburn, who had joined the team as its chief scientific advisor and vaccine lead, respectively, in May. This was subsequent to Dr. Birx's unfortunate and inappropriate dressing down of Peter in the White House Situation Room.

Whereas Peter was most interested in some of the early clinical trial data emerging from the vaccines under development, Moncef took a much more comprehensive and strategic approach to establishing the slate of candidates, which we would nurture and in which we would eventually invest.

He knew all the leading vaccine development companies and their senior executives. He thought ahead to how to create the greatest probability of achieving our objective: at least one safe and effective vaccine, including effectiveness in those over age sixty-five, able to obtain EUA approval, and manufactured at scale all by year's end at the latest.

From here, he methodically evaluated the early data and presented a slate of six, with the potential of a seventh, vaccine candidates. His selection of six cut across three different vaccine technologies, each having advantages and disadvantages but collectively representing our highest probability of success.

While we were completely enamored with Moncef's ability to think strategically, we decided that a little bit of trust but verify at this point was in order. Accordingly, in late August, with support from one of our advisors, Chan Harjivan, we took the six vaccine candidates and evaluated them against the most important criteria: the ability to complete a clinical trial and obtain an EUA before the end of the year, whether or not it would be effective in those over age sixty-five, and whether it could be manufactured at scale with some degree of confidence, again by year's end.

We independently and in confidence approached different members of the team. We asked each to assess the probabilities of each of the six candidates meeting the three criteria. Then we separately conducted a cumulative probability analysis, revealing the following: Moncef's slate of candidates had a 75 percent probability of producing at least one safe and effective vaccine manufactured at scale and authorized by the FDA by January 2021, a 35 percent chance of having two or more vaccines meeting these criteria, and less than a 10 percent probability of having three (see the exhibit on page 59). This bolstered our confidence.

It also revealed where the team could put incremental resources to get the highest return possible on increasing the probability of success. From our analysis, the area where this return on management time would be greatest was in accelerating the clinical trial outcomes.

Even in the earliest days of Operation Warp Speed, determining the slate of candidates eligible for government support was the area of greatest uncertainty. Moncef described settling on a slate of vaccine candidates as one of the highlights of his time at OWS.[5] He knew enough about the slate to realize we now had a high probability of success, and we had just confirmed it with a completely independent analysis.

Why not invest in twenty candidates, some may ask. Funding was not an issue. President Trump had already assured us he would obtain whatever funding was necessary, and Secretary Mnuchin had already established the fact that the US economy, running at half-speed, cost several billion dollars *per day* in forgone federal tax revenue. Thus, the economic return on investment alone, not to mention the number of lives saved, associated with delivering a successful vaccine a year or two early was almost infinite.

The answer to limiting the slate of vaccine candidates to no more than six or seven really lay deeper into things money could not buy as easily: leadership time and attention, availability of raw materials produced mainly overseas, the potential limitations of how many Americans would enroll in clinical trials, and the severity of the COVID outbreak necessary to validate the clinical trial outcomes. Strategy experts often advise that strategy is as much about what one does *not* do as it is about what one chooses to do. Dr. Slaoui and General Perna both understood this. Our slate of candidates remained at six. This disciplined strategic thinking was absolutely essential to our eventual success.

Vaccines: Scenario planning for priority candidates

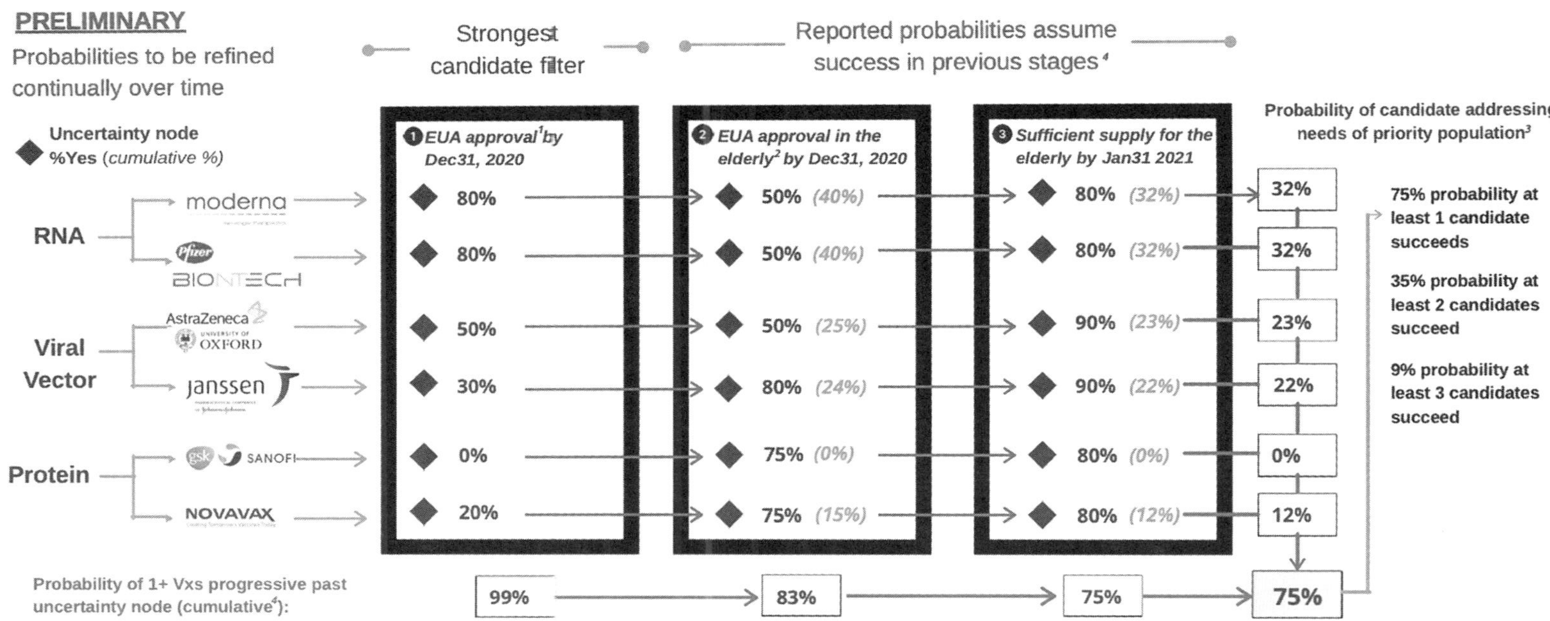

1. Emergency use authorization for the initial clinical trial population 2. Emergency use authorization for the elderly defined as 65 years or older 3. EUA approval in the general population for the general population by December 2020, the elderly by December 2020 and sufficient supply to treat the elderly by January 2021 4. Reported values assume the probabilities across each candidate are independent of the others (higher bound), which may not be accurate (especially within the same platform) 5. For example, stage 2 probabilities report the likelihood that a Vx candidate receives EUA approval in the elderly

4

THE MONEY AND THE SCIENCE

OBTAINING FUNDING FOR THE VACCINE CANDIDATES

Funding all aspects of Operation Warp Speed would cost approximately $30 billion.

But this sum did not cover all aspects of President Trump's pledge that every American would be vaccinated free of charge. This meant no out-of-pocket obligation for those being vaccinated, not even the fee of the nurse or other health care worker who administered the injection. We needed to cover both.

When the vaccines came available, the commercial insurance industry graciously decided it would waive any patient charges for

COVID-19 vaccinations,[1] and its members would reimburse vaccinators at normal rates.

The Coronavirus Aid, Relief, and Economic Security (CARES) Act, which passed by Congress in March, had already increased the overall percentage of state Medicaid expenses funded by the federal government. That covered COVID-related Medicaid costs where there were little or no payments by patients in the first place.[2]

My HHS colleague Jim Parker worked with the leaders at the Center for Medicare and Medicaid Services (CMS) to waive patient co-pays for vaccinations in the Medicare fee-for-service program. We turned to the Provider Relief Fund, created under the COVID relief CARES Act passed in March to reimburse providers for those without any insurance. Tom Engels, who was the administrator of the Health Resource and Services Administration (HRSA), the agency overseeing the distribution of the Provider Relief Fund, was instrumental in making this happen.

Still, we needed to come up with the $30 billion to fund the core Operation Warp Speed program.

The Office of Management and Budget (OMB) at the White House is one of the most powerful and influential bodies in the entire federal government. Virtually all aspects of administrative rulemaking, the president's budget, relationships with congressional appropriators, and general support for any administration's priorities flow through the political appointees and their career officials there. In many administrations, contentious relationships develop between departments, such as HHS and officials at OMB.

Fortunately, this was not the case in 2020. Before the pandemic, there was an unusual arrangement in which the acting chief of staff to the president, Mick Mulvaney, was also the director of OMB. His deputy, Russ Vought was largely directing the agency during this time, and then Russ became the acting director when Mick left. Russ's health-care division program associate director was Greg D'Angelo, the key person at OMB supporting OWS.

Greg D'Angelo was born and raised in New Jersey and went off to

Duke University after high school to earn his degree in political science and public policy. He had originally anticipated studying math while there, but only weeks after he had started his time at Duke as a freshman, we were attacked by terrorists on September 11, 2001.

This is when he decided he had to get involved with public policy. After graduation in 2005, he initially thought about going straight to law school but decided instead to take an internship at the American Enterprise Institute (AEI) under the tutelage of former speaker of the House Newt Gingrich.

At the time, Speaker Gingrich was spending a good deal of time on the topic of health care, so Greg both learned a lot and became interested in health care from a policy perspective as well. Gingrich successfully talked him out of law school, and Greg went on to earn his master's degree in health policy from Johns Hopkins University while working at the Heritage Foundation. During the Obamacare debates in 2009–2010, he was recruited to the Senate Budget Committee under the leadership of Senator Judd Gregg, which enhanced his knowledge of health care.

While he was interested in joining the Trump administration in early 2017, he was also needed in the Senate role to help usher through the "repeal and replace" of the Affordable Care Act. When that failed, he stayed until the Congress passed President Trump's tax bill, and then he moved over to OMB in early 2019.[3]

Shortly after Greg joined OMB, I moved up from chief of staff at the Center for Medicare and Medicaid Services (CMS) to fill the HHS deputy chief of staff for policy role. Greg and I established a close relationship very quickly. This relationship extended to Secretary Azar as well, so there was a significant degree of trust on both sides, which served us all well thereafter.

Greg's deep understanding of how congressional appropriations worked, his contacts on the Hill, and his knowledge of health care soon became invaluable to the challenge of funding OWS. But then we still needed to get past the newly appointed White House chief of staff, Mark Meadows.

"Chief" Meadows has a way of commanding a room. Born in France to the son of an active-duty US Army service member, he was reared in Brandon, Florida. He earned his college degree from the University of South Florida and shortly thereafter entered the restaurant and land development businesses in North Carolina.

He became active in North Carolina politics during this period, before running and winning a seat in Congress. Ushered in with the emerging Tea Party movement in 2012, Meadows built a reputation as a bona fide conservative and was the founding member of the Freedom Caucus in Congress.

He was also an avid defender and supporter of the president from the floor of the House, before being asked to become the White House chief of staff. When dealing with Congress in his new role, he was always thinking a few steps ahead and reasoning back as one would do on a chess board.[4]

There was no question he was a shrewd politician. He quickly and effectively consolidated White House decision-making under his authority. We observed this firsthand with the $175 billion that, in March, Congress allocated through the CARES Act to the Provider Relief Fund. Not a penny of that money, which was technically allocated to Secretary Azar, was spent without Meadows's approval. Needless to say, Meadows made all final Operation Warp Speed funding decisions: how much would we get, from where would it come, and at what point in time it would be released.

The backdrop to all of this was the "cat and mouse" game going on up on Capitol Hill over the next supplement to the COVID funding relief bill. During the summer and fall of 2020, Speaker Pelosi was adhering to her political desire to delay COVID funding until after the November election (to deny the president credit for meeting the emergency) against the urgent need to fight a rapidly spreading and destructive pandemic, including developing and deploying vaccines.

Chief Meadows and Russ Vought from OMB were the principal negotiators from our side. We, in OWS, needed to develop contingencies to the likelihood that Pelosi would continue to deny funding until after the election, which, of course, she ultimately did.[5] Under no circumstances, did Meadows wish to ask Pelosi for more Warp Speed funding during this negotiation. It would have cost leverage. We turned to a time-honored Washington activity: find funds by (legally) reallocating existing appropriations.

By late August, as Dr. Slaoui and General Perna were finalizing the slate of vaccine candidates in which the government would invest, we were quickly exhausting all the obvious funding options from within HHS. BARDA had been allocated several billion dollars in the CARES Act for medical countermeasure funding. The CDC had received some, too. The NIH had received some to accelerate the development of COVID-related diagnostics. And the Strategic National Stockpile, under Assistant Secretary Kadlec had some funding as well. Jen Moughalian, the very capable HHS CFO, was fond of saying, "We can continue to look under the couch cushions for a little more," but there was no possible means of getting to the target of $30 billion.

The time was right for a "financial summit" with the White House. Greg D'Angelo and Russ Vought organized a meeting with Chief Meadows in his office for all of us to discuss.

Meadows's office is just down the hall from the Oval Office. The traditional chief of staff's office was expansive by West Wing standards but, of course, smaller than the president's and vice president's suites.

It had a desk, flanked by a large conference table at one end of the room, and a sitting area on the other. As with every other office in the White House, there were a couple of television monitors constantly displaying different news channels. Jared Kushner's office was closer to the Oval Office but significantly smaller than the chief of staff's. We all gathered in Meadow's sitting area and got down to business.

There were a couple of obvious accounts from which we could legally "borrow" (such as the Provider Relief Fund) or take (such as the multiple billions of dollars of unspent surplus from the approximately $25 billion earmarked for COVID testing left over from other parts of the CARES Act).[6]

In ninety minutes, led principally by Meadows and D'Angelo, we laid out the sources, amounts, and timing of Operation Warp Speed funds. We carefully adhered to what our legal authorizations permitted us to do but in ways that would not require congressional notification and thereby disrupt the ongoing negotiations with the Hill. Meadows wanted to ensure that we could get through the August recess before we had to notify Congress that we had dipped into any other funding.

At the conclusion of the meeting, Greg and I were sent back to his office across the way in the Eisenhower Executive Office Building to "work out the details."[7] We came up with about $17 billion to be allocated roughly two-thirds for vaccine development and manufacturing and one-third to fund the distribution of the vaccines.

We also decided that the funding organization for all of Operation Warp Speed's investments in vaccines and related supplies would be the Biomedical Advanced Research and Development Authority (BARDA), which was under the leadership of Gary Disbrow and Robert Johnson, both of whom we trusted.

This single source of funding precluded the typical squabbles that occur between and among government agencies and ensured we could direct the moneys quickly, based on the Operation Warp Speed board's decisions. The Department of Defense, accustomed to engaging in multiple billions of dollars of contracts each year, provided much needed contracting capacity support, enabling us to get everything done quickly with a minimum of fuss.

From that point forward, Jen Moughalian, Greg D'Angelo, and I conducted weekly coordination meetings to ensure everything remained within budget. But we never again encountered a financial constraint in getting the job done, a little-known reason for the success of Operation Warp Speed. Credit belongs to the collective creativity of Meadows, Vought, D'Angelo, and Moughalian.

THE PIVOTAL ROLE OF DR. FRANCIS COLLINS

Throughout Operation Warp Speed, Dr. Collins played a key, usually behind the scenes, role. This was particularly true in the success of our phase III clinical trials program.

One of the most significant challenges we faced was organizing, staging, and completing the phase III clinical trials. Phase I clinical trials typically involve a relatively small number (30–40) humans essentially to determine safety (i.e., are there any bad side effects?). Phase II clinical trials typically involve a couple of hundred humans to determine effectiveness (i.e., does the treatment work?), assess the dose levels needed to be effective, and continue to monitor safety. Phase III clinical trials are the final test before FDA authorization or approval and typically involve hundreds, if not thousands, of human participants. In the case of COVID vaccine phase III trials, the FDA established that the minimum number of enrollees would be 30,000 per vaccine candidate.[8]

In late March and early April 2020, the NIH, at Dr. Collins's initiative, formed a scientific leadership group. The group eventually included as many as twenty chief scientific officers from the pharmaceutical companies most relevant to the fight against COVID. He dubbed it "ACTIV," an acronym for "Accelerating COVID-19 Therapeutic Interventions and Vaccines."

ACTIV evolved into a public-private partnership to coordinate research. It built upon the collaborative effort called "Accelerating Medicines Project," or AMP, initiated by Collins and the NIH in 2014. The AMP concept was simple: the NIH would share research costs fifty-fifty with commercial companies that would use the combined funds to focus on developing the medicines most needed for highly prevalent diseases, such as diabetes and Alzheimer's.[9]

This foundation of trust, and the relationship bonds, created over many years before the onset of COVID proved vital to the collaboration that followed. While Secretary Azar was busy setting up Operation Warp Speed in early April, Dr. Collins was forming the ACTIV group. He conducted his first call with participants on April 3, with a formal kickoff on April 17.

Within ACTIV, Dr. Collins formed the Vaccine Working Group (VWG). VWG's principal function would be to establish master protocols for the upcoming phase III vaccine clinical trials. Collins invited Peter Marks, by then back full time as director of the Center for Biologics Evaluation and Research (CBER), to be an integral part of this working group. Drawing upon his favorable experience with collaboration, Collins wanted to ensure that all parties were fully aligned on the protocols. Three fundamental decisions eventually emanated from this group.

First, the clinical trials would need a minimum of 30,000 participants. This would be significantly higher than the 20,000 normally required to license a vaccine, but the team wanted to emphasize that we were not going to compromise any aspect of quality or safety.

Second, this group defined the clinical trial endpoints, the standard for gauging the level of a vaccine's effectiveness. As an endpoint for the COVID vaccines to be evaluated by the FDA, the working group settled it would *not* be the presence of the virus in any given individual after inoculation, but whether the individual experienced "symptomatic illness."[10]

In other words, the group wanted to evaluate effectiveness of the vaccines, not on whether they prevented infection but whether they would prevent serious illness.

This is the meaning of the metric most Americans remember for the Pfizer and Moderna vaccines as being "95 percent effective." It meant that out of all phase III trial participants testing positive for COVID and experiencing serious symptoms more than fourteen days after inoculation, 95 percent had received the placebo, and 5 percent had received the vaccine represented.

Third, the group decided that a single Data and Safety Monitoring Board (DSMB), would be shared among the vaccine candidates going through the trials.[11] With roughly thirteen members (independent scientists from appropriate fields), the DSMB played a critical role in providing objective evaluation of the trials.

After finding a predetermined number of infections, the DSMB had the authority to stop a trial and declare the vaccine either ineffective or effective enough to seek EUA approval. Or it could declare the data inconclusive and order the trial to continue until more conclusive data emerged. Having a shared DSMB among the companies going through vaccine trials helped ensure consistency.

That summer, following these initial meetings, Peter Marks and the FDA issued guidance regarding phase III clinical trials. They reinforced the key parameter of 30,000 participants of sufficient diversity as the minimum number necessary to determine both the safety and effectiveness profile of a COVID-19 vaccine.[12] The NIH's Vaccine Working Group and the FDA were completely aligned on this.

One question posed repeatedly to Dr. Slaoui and the team was, "Why not engage in human challenge studies?" Human challenge studies require intentionally infecting healthy people with the virus to see if the vaccine, in this case, would be effective. While the approach may have sped up determining the effectiveness of the vaccines, it may not have been sufficient to understand the vaccine's safety profile.

It also raised obvious ethical questions. We would have had to insert the COVID virus deep into the subjects' lungs, in persons over age sixty-five, knowing that the fatality rate in this age group was relatively high, and no meaningfully effective therapeutic (cure) was available to treat those who got sick. In other words, there was high probability that we would end up sacrificing some lives in the hope of saving others.

Dr. Slaoui expressed strong convictions about the morality of human challenge studies. His logic was again compelling. Fewer than 1 percent of individuals infected with COVID in the community would die, while over 99 percent survived. As well, we had no effective therapeutics at the time to help those whom a human challenge study would intentionally infect. Why would we knowingly wind up sacrificing elderly Americans in a trial when these were the probabilities? Dr. Collins backed him up. We decided against human challenge studies.

By the fall of 2020, there was one other factor contributing to this decision: the widespread outbreak of COVID-19 infections across many parts of the country. Given the intensity of the outbreaks, we believed a standard trial of 30,000-plus individuals would reveal a vaccine's safety and efficacy profile soon enough.

A "STRATEGIC INTERVENTION" WITH MODERNA

There were immense challenges associated with conducting multiple clinical trials comprising 30,000+ individuals each simultaneously. The National Institutes for Health (NIH) is expert at organizing and conducting such trials, as are the well-known clinical research organizations (CROs), which organize trials for pharmaceutical companies and on which we depended heavily for staging and conducting COVID-19 clinical trials. These trials posed specific and unique challenges relative to typical drug trials.

For example, in cancer trials, the participants are known well in advance. The trial sites are, by and large, well-established academic medical centers to which patients might travel significant distances to enroll. Time-constraints are not a major concern for the most part. In contrast, for COVID-19 vaccine trials, we needed to anticipate where outbreaks would occur and then quickly set up trial sites near where those likely to be infected lived and worked.

Also, given how the virus was differentially affecting persons of various ages, genders, underlying clinical conditions, and possibly race, the numbers of participants needed to be significantly larger than typical drug trials. The trials needed to incorporate a high level of demographic diversity.

Qualifying as an approved site in a large-scale human clinical trial requires exacting preparation, processes, and training. It involves Institutional Review Board (IRB) approval, setting up the actual sites, developing detailed contracts for lawyers to approve and enrollees to sign, recruiting enrollees, collecting copious amounts of information from those subjects, and tracking the subjects long after they receive their injections. Under Dr. Collins's and Dr. Fauci's leadership, the task of organizing all of this fell to Dr. John Mascola.

Throughout Operation Warp Speed, John Mascola was the director of the Vaccine Research Center within NIAID, of which Dr. Fauci was the head. Mascola was one of the Center's founders when it opened in 2000. He received his undergraduate degree from Tufts University and his medical degree from the Georgetown University School of Medicine.

After his residency, he completed multiple fellowships in infectious diseases. Great scientific work led to his election to the National Academy of Medicine in 2017. He served as Tony Fauci's right-hand man throughout the pandemic and was pivotal to the success of the vaccine clinical trials.[13] One of Dr. Mascola's key tasks was to work with Dr. Hepburn, our vaccine lead, and others on the Operation Warp Speed team, to anticipate where the next set of severe US COVID-19 outbreaks would arise.

In the early summer, the number of American COVID cases dropped as the weather got hotter. We began developing contingencies for staging some of the clinical trials in places such as Brazil, which was entering its cooler seasons and seeing its caseload rise. But soon with Memorial Day, and then Labor Day, travel reignited outbreaks in the US. The result was that we would establish a sufficient number of clinical trial sites, participants, and, eventually, positive cases here to get the job done at home.

But whether done at home or abroad, selecting optimal sites (i.e., where we could expect large-scale outbreaks within a matter of weeks) was critical to the pace at which we could determine the efficacy of the trial vaccines. Matt Hepburn, along with one of our advisors, Chan Harjivan, collaborated closely with Dr. Mascola on this effort. Matt and Chan would review the leading indicators (e.g., test positivity rate, change in test positivity rate, density of population, degree of mitigation efforts) by county and suggest additional trial sites. John Mascola would then work with the clinical research organizations to add sites to the related trial.

For many logistical and other reasons, we made the decision that no vaccine clinical trial site would be a site for more than one vaccine candidate at a time. As one can imagine, however, this further complicated the task of selecting sites. Again, we needed to anticipate, as noted above, where the outbreaks of the virus would be many weeks in advance of opening the trial itself.

As discussed previously, each of these trials is overseen by an independent body known as the Data and Safety Monitoring Board (DSMB), comprising a cross-section of medical professionals who review infection data to which the vaccine developer is "blind." The board reveals the data once an agreed-upon level of statistical significance is reached. For all manufacturers except Pfizer, there was a shared DSMB.

The Moderna and Pfizer phase III clinical trials kicked off on July 30 and July 31, respectively. This coincided with the post-Independence Day increase in viral spread, which was becoming evident. It produced a paradox for all of us: we desperately wanted to keep the virus under control until we obtained a safe and effective vaccine manufactured at scale, yet to obtain that vaccine, we needed Americans enrolled in the trial to become infected.

The NIH, under Dr. Lawrence Corey, committed its HIV/AIDS clinical trial sites to assist with the COVID-19 trials, and these eventually comprised about one-third of Moderna's sites.[14] The other two-thirds were set up by a contract research organization (CRO), a third-party organization specializing in setting up trial sites, recruiting participants, and helping to collect data from the participants.[15] Each set of sites was held to the same, very strict protocols and standards.

As Moderna entered the late stages its phase III clinical trials, one aspect of the data on its trial participants came into focus: the lack of demographic diversity. The virus seemed to be affecting some populations more severely, making their relatively limited representation in the trial populations a rising concern as we approached the end of August 2020.

We had agreed on the priority of verifying that the vaccine was effective in those most affected by the virus. For instance, if the vaccine was not effective in those over age sixty-five, due perhaps to the diminished strength of immune response generally found in the elderly, then the vaccine would not help a group very vulnerable to either hospitalization or death from contracting the virus. Poor results among the elderly to Merck's vaccine ultimately prompted the company to withdraw from the program.

Near the end of August, we recognized Moderna's problem: the company was approximately one month into its phase III clinical trial. Enrollment was going spectacularly well in terms of aggregate numbers. However, the desired diversity of enrollees was sorely lacking, which could have nullified the entire trial. It was at this point that Dr. Collins intervened.

Starting on Saturday, August 29, and continuing on Saturdays for weeks thereafter, Dr. Collins assembled on a conference call Moderna's senior executive team and the appropriate clinical trial site leaders. Every Saturday morning was devoted to discussing how Moderna, with the assistance of NIH, could enhance minority recruiting.[16] Tony Fauci and Moncef Slaoui participated in these calls. Dr. Jerome Adams, the surgeon general, who is African American, lent significant support and passion to these sessions. We were targeting a minimum of 10 percent participation each among blacks and Hispanics, as well as a minimum of 25 percent for those over age sixty-five.

At a couple of points in the process, we considered shutting down all recruiting except in minority populations. We all believed achieving statistical significance in trial participation for these minorities would be critical to enhancing vaccine confidence within these groups. Then, too, the FDA, and ultimately the CDC's Advisory Committee on Immunization Practices (ACIP), would certainly need to be comfortable with the diversity of the clinical trial participants before granting emergency use authorization and then prioritization for use within these groups.

At first, Moderna seemed only to "tolerate" these sessions. Dr. Collins, who is not prone to anger, had to play the bad cop a couple of times. But before long, Moderna's executives not only embraced these sessions and their objective but brought new ideas to the group for evaluation. Stephane Bancel, Moderna's CEO and two of his executives, Melanie Iverson, the chief development officer, and Stephen Hoge, who was Moderna's president, participated actively and were eventually instrumental in successfully diversifying the trial participants.

More than anyone at the NIH, Francis Collins was all in when it came to advancing the objectives of Operation Warp Speed. He always had his facts straight, was constantly engaged, rarely missed a single morning "synch-up" session, all the while leading ACTIV and directing the NIH. In retrospect, the decision by the Trump administration to keep this Obama appointee on-board as NIH director proved a godsend. The relationships and trust he had developed over a decade were crucial to the pace at which we advanced the Operation Warp Speed public-private partnership.

5

MAKING IT

EXPANDING MANUFACTURING CAPACITY

In the spring of 2020, there was virtually no excess vaccine production capacity in the United States.[1] The Operation Warp Speed team, with the benefit of Carlo de Notaristefani's vast experience and leadership, eventually helped set up or expanded twenty-seven vaccine manufacturing facilities all over the country.[2]

To do this, Moncef and Carlo decided that a *product team* organization was required to meet our goals.[3] A product team is a small group of specialists who together have all the skills needed to get a job done, in this case setting up an advanced pharmaceutical plant and getting it producing at the highest volume to the highest global standards.

We tapped the best people for our tasks at NIH, BARDA, and the Army, including seven field-grade officers. These officers formed the nucleus of a concept Carlo referred to as "persons in plants." We deployed them all over the country. Each spent ten to twelve hours per day in the factories we were setting up or expanding. These "persons in plants" gave us a comprehensive picture of what was happening minute-to-minute in each plant. The exception was Pfizer, which refused to work with our team. Then we, and the nation paid a price for this peculiar resistance when Pfizer failed to deliver on its contracted numbers of doses in November and December.

The product teams, or more formally, product coordination teams (PCT), served another very important purpose. Outside of the FDA, no one in the federal government was permitted to contact or interact with the manufacturer without the PCT leader knowing about it. The NIH, CDC, BARDA, members of the Strategic National Stockpile, and other members of the Operation Warp Speed team all had legitimate reasons to interact with the manufacturers. It could have become impossibly confusing and time-consuming for all involved if communications were not coordinated and funneled through the respective PCT leader. This process discipline produced a quick, clear, helpful flow of information within and between plants with a maximum of signal (useful information and discussion) and a minimum of noise (the opposite).

At first, the agencies within Health and Human Services resisted deployment of their professionals to Operation Warp Speed PCTs without a reporting relationship back to their home agency. That did not last long. Two critical requirements imposed by Moncef Slaoui quickly transformed this disparate group of professionals into a single cohesive team.

First, he required multi-hour, in-person meetings for both vaccines and therapeutics each week. These occurred during months when most federal employees were still working from home. These meetings were conducted in a large third-floor conference room in the Humphrey

Building and typically had fifteen to twenty participants. The tables were set in a U-shaped format. General Perna and Dr. Slaoui sat at a corner where two tables came together. This permitted them to have side conversations without disrupting the larger discussion in the room.

When General Perna entered the room, military and civilian rose out of respect. But these were not hierarchical meetings—just the opposite. Every team member was treated as a peer. The purpose was simple and direct: surface every issue, engage all with relevant skills and experience to evaluate it, and agree on what to do and who to do it.

General Perna was particularly skilled at putting subordinates at ease. Dr. Slaoui was also masterful in these meetings—always strategic, always two or three steps ahead of the group but in a manner that facilitated discussion, not stifling it.

He would sit and listen attentively for what could be ten to fifteen minutes of back-and-forth. Then he would intercede, pulling together disparate points, injecting his own logic, and offering what invariably became a course of action.

He always had the complete slate of vaccine candidates in mind. He was always thinking through the potential relationships among several clinical trials. He completely understood where we were with respect to manufacturing progress, timing of clinical trials, and submission of applications for emergency use authorizations (EUAs).

The second requirement Dr. Slaoui imposed was simple but transformative. When someone in the room would refer to himself as a member of his originating organization (e.g., BARDA, NIH, CDC), he would interrupt and say, "You meant to say you are a member of the Operation Warp Speed Team." Everyone got the message instantly. This was not a task force represented by multiple agencies, it was a single, integrated team whose members needed to subscribe to a new identity.

Every manufacturing plant needed some sort of retrofitting, which required new equipment, much of which was manufactured outside the United States. Instead of waiting weeks for trans-oceanic delivery, General Perna ordered contracted US military planes to places such as

France, Germany, and Belgium to secure the specialized equipment and fly it back to the United States in hours. Once in the US, General Perna's team often coordinated with the Department of Transportation, so oversized trucks could use our interstate highways to move the equipment to its final destination without delays. Even over the Independence and Labor Day weekends in 2020, these massive trucks were on the road.[4] The team took no holidays. We never forgot that days wasted were counted in lives lost.

Every single step in construction and plant qualification was entered into a master schedule managed by the Department of Defense and our custom-designed software application, Tiberius. Whenever a problem emerged, we knew about it immediately and deployed resources to resolve it.

From decades of experience, Carlo knew that starting up a plant, or even an additional production line in an existing plant, always involved surprises, challenges, problems, and barriers. The key was to surface these early and address them immediately. On Christmas Eve 2020, for instance, we flew in technicians from Europe to fix a problem.

Carlo divided the task of expanding manufacturing capacity into three major components: a properly designed, constructed, and equipped facility; adequate supplies and raw materials; and skilled labor.

He urged us to peer deeply into each. For example, he said that to understand the supply chain, we had to understand the constraints not just on our suppliers, but on our suppliers' suppliers and even our suppliers' suppliers' suppliers. To illustrate, he estimated that more than fifty percent of the raw materials we needed for successful vaccine manufacturing had to come from *outside* the United States. Understanding this kind of analysis, General Perna had a team of experts operating out of the Vaccine Operations Center (VOC) on the second floor of the Humphrey Building (HHS headquarters), tracking the flow of vaccine-related supplies daily from each of these suppliers. Again and again, when a situation requiring attention emerged, Carlo and his team were all over it.

Obtaining and training skilled labor to work the manufacturing facilities was one of our most challenging tasks. The pandemic had already shut down many US manufacturing facilities, and we were trying to hire thousands of skilled employees. During this period alone, Catalent, just one of the major vaccine manufacturers with which we were working, increased its vaccine workforce from approximately 400 to over 2000.[5] Emergent, another of our manufacturers, started with 120 but soon needed 500. In most cases where we experienced manufacturing quality challenges, the lack of trained, or experienced, labor was the root cause. Of course, we had the assistance of one other key lever at our disposal: the Defense Production Act.

INVOKING THE DEFENSE PRODUCTION ACT

In 1950, to ensure that during national crises, industry gave proper priority to the defense needs of the nation, Congress enacted the Defense Production Act (DPA). The DPA empowers the president, largely through executive order, to direct private companies to "allocate materials, services, and facilities" for national defense purposes, as determined by the president.[6] Very importantly, it shields companies from lawsuits when compliance hurts other customers and permits companies under DPA orders to compel *those in their own supply chains* all the way back to raw materials to put the orders for the government first. The DPA originally applied only to US companies, but over the years, reciprocal agreements had been concluded with a number of allies, notably Canada.

Title 1 of the DPA deals with priorities and allocations. It is governed by the Defense Priorities and Allocations system (DPAS), which is administered by the Department of Commerce. In 1996, an executive order extended the DPA's authorities to include health-related resources, and a parallel process known as the Health Resources Priorities and Allocations System (HRPAS) was created.[7]

We used the DPA authorities eighteen separate times to prioritize delivery of raw materials, industrial equipment, consumable supplies, and even to prioritize skilled labor.[8] In the context of a global pandemic already constraining supply chains, this leverage proved essential to our successful expansion of vaccine manufacturing capacity.

Our eighteen uses of the DPA were wide-ranging. For instance, we used it so Corning Inc. could expand its vaccine glass vial and tubing capacity. The supply chain provision enabled all six of our vaccine candidate manufacturers to receive immediate access to raw materials, critical equipment, and repair parts. And we used it in support of Cytiva, a company manufacturing many of the consumables (e.g., filters, special bags) associated with vaccine production.[9]

Approving DPA and HRPAS requests was one of the key functions of the Operation Warp Speed board, and the board members took this responsibility very seriously. Deputy Department of Defense Secretary David Norquist often represented Secretary Esper at these meetings. He always wanted to know how invoking the DPA authorities would impact and disrupt other aspects of the nation's COVID response. The members of the Army Material Command, under General Perna, were experts at understanding US industry supply chains and spent lots of time analyzing the impact on them before advancing a request to the Operation Warp Speed board.

The only problem we encountered among our eighteen uses of the DPA was with Pfizer. It is hard to know for sure, but politics may have been at least partially behind Pfizer's generally difficult stance toward OWS, even while depending heavily on our assistance with packaging, distributing, and administering its doses. Greek by birth, the CEO, Albert Bourla, made no secret of his anger over the president's pressure on drug companies to lower their prices.[10]

In any event, the DPA imposes very specific requirements on companies seeking authority to bring a supplier under the law's umbrella. Those requirements include answering such questions as: What supplies do you need? From what suppliers? In what quantities? Over what period? For use in what products or services?

For a long time, Pfizer declined to answer these questions yet voiced frustration with not receiving a priority rating under the DPA. We speculated that the company intended to use the DPA to help it manufacture vaccines that would be shipped overseas, which, in many cases, the DPA prohibited. In the late fall, Pfizer began to encounter serious raw material and spare parts constraints. Only then did it comply with the DPA's requirements and receive (in December) a priority rating.[11]

RAMPING UP VACCINE MANUFACTURING

In manufacturing the vaccines, as with all aspects of Operation Warp Speed, we engaged many companies (12) with many production sites (27). If one site or company failed, we had others to fall back on.

For example, in vaccine development, one company (Merck) ultimately gave up. Another (Sanofi/GSK) did not anticipate delivering doses until at least the fall of 2021. But two developers delivered authorized vaccines in December 2020, and one more in February 2021.

In manufacturing, we engaged twelve highly experienced pharmaceutical production companies. They devoted a total of twenty-seven facilities to COVID vaccine production. After normal start-up pains, twenty-six facilities performed brilliantly. One failed.

The media was rightly interested in our manufacturing story. The closer we were to the initial EUA approvals, the greater the interest in how we would be making the doses. Never before had so many vaccine-making facilities been established or expanded simultaneously. By early fall, plants from South Texas to the Research Triangle in North Carolina, to Indianapolis, and to Baltimore began producing batches of vaccines, in some cases with output numbering in the millions of doses.[12]

Still, as Carlo told us again and again, he could not remember a single instance in his vaccine manufacturing career when a start-up of production did *not* encounter significant glitches. Drug manufacturers, he explained, are meticulous about perfecting each step in the process. However, when all these steps are assembled into a single integrated manufacturing *system,* and the system is stressed suddenly and all at once, weak points emerge. Often, perhaps almost always, the system fails. No matter how effective each step is on its own, he would remind us, activating the system, as a system, reveals the almost inevitable points of failure.[13] His rule: to maintain quality standards without compromise, we needed to rapidly identify and then address failures as they emerged.

As an example, one of our manufacturers designed a complex process control panel for its bulk production facility and had a Swiss firm produce it. This panel failed in the middle of the night on six consecutive batches, which led to several weeks of investigation, evaluation, and problem-solving. In the end, the cause of the failure was a simple electrical grounding issue.

A second example: Another manufacturer experienced a sterility issue, introduced, it turned out, by a vial supplier. The sterility testing was conducted only in the UK. We had to pull out all stops to first get new samples to the testing laboratory, and then to have our testing prioritized before we could resume fulfilling orders, which in this case involved hundreds of thousands of doses.

A third manufacturer made the decision to "scale out" rather than "scale up." So instead of increasing its capacity of *existing lines* of production, it simply expanded from one, to eight, to, eventually, forty-eight lines. Each of these lines needed to be validated independently, which created such a delay that the manufacturer had to import finished goods from Europe to meet its production commitments.[14]

The instability of these manufacturing processes is precisely why General Perna and the entire OWS team decided in December and early January to hold second doses in inventory until the three- or four-week intervals for second-dose administration had passed. We were criticized for not distributing all doses from inventory right away, but we had made a public promise that there would be second doses available to anyone who had received a first dose. With the instability of manufacturing processes in the early weeks, the only way we could be sure of meeting this obligation was by keeping the second doses in reserve until they could be administered as second doses.

In the spring and early summer of 2021, one of our manufacturers, Emergent, received a lot of media attention and rightly so.[15] Emergent was in part a reserve asset of the US government. The government paid the company to maintain idle vaccine production lines, so it would have the *option* of turning on that capacity in the event of a pandemic or a bioterror attack. The company received funding annually to keep this capacity available even if it were unused.

It was a good and prudent concept, but it turned out that Carlo's "iron law of start-up glitches" also applied to idle capacity, maybe particularly to idle capacity if that capacity had not been actively manufacturing for a while.[16] This was the case with the Emergent Baltimore plant.

Carlo conducted an assessment of Emergent in the late summer of 2020 and found deficiencies. This was not surprising in and of itself, but what was surprising was management's lack of response to our findings of shortcomings. Carlo described it as "watching a slow-motion train wreck."[17] Emergent had established production contracts directly with Johnson & Johnson and AstraZeneca, so our ability to influence the company was limited.

When we identified employee training issues in Emergent's Baltimore facility, we discussed them with the executive leadership team there. Again, its response was lethargic. We even raised these issues with the vaccine developers, which had contracted with Emergent—J&J and AstraZeneca—but they believed they could get the situation under control.

In the spring of 2021, when all the warning signals proved right and Emergent experienced serious quality control issues from cross-contamination, J&J had to take over management of the site.[18] Given our funding in support of both J&J and AstraZeneca, this is one instance where we should have asserted our will far more strongly.

HELP FROM THE DEPARTMENT OF JUSTICE

As discussed earlier, vaccine manufacturing capacity was scarce in the spring of 2020. In some cases, this was the result of a few companies having excess capacity but deciding not to compete to manufacture COVID-19 vaccines, while others who were developing vaccines had no manufacturing capacity available at all. The same was true for therapeutics manufacturing. But was such collaboration legal under the antitrust laws? In June 2020, representatives from the Department of Justice (DOJ) contacted Carlo to discuss this issue.[19]

Several weeks later, on July 23, the DOJ's Antitrust Division issued a letter under the signature of Assistant Attorney General Makan Delrahim. It described how the DOJ would permit competitors to collaborate in support of the public health emergency and objectives of the COVID-19 pandemic response. Originally intended to enable more therapeutics manufacturing, the principles articulated in the letter applied to vaccine production, too.

DOJ recognized the need in the COVID emergency for competing companies to exchange information in three critical areas of manufacturing. Normally, the companies would have been subject to anti-trust scrutiny but not after the DOJ released its letter.

The DOJ letter permitted the sharing of vital information:

- Technical details regarding relevant manufacturing facilities, including total potential capacity, technical specifications, time periods during which facilities would be available, and who owned the facility;
- Technical information regarding manufacturing processes and platforms;
- Information regarding the sources and amounts of available raw materials and supplies necessary to manufacture the specific product.

DOJ wisely precluded any exchange of information regarding prices or commercial arrangements for raw materials and supplies and placed other safeguards, such as limiting the duration of such information exchange only to "as long as necessary to address the Covid-19 crisis."[20]

Carlo would assert that this policy on the part of the DOJ was instrumental in rapidly expanding vaccine production capacity in late

2020 and into 2021. It resulted in arrangements between Moderna and Sanofi, J&J and Sanofi, and J&J and Merck.

For example, in March 2021, having dropped out of the vaccine race in January, Merck made an agreement with Johnson & Johnson to manufacture J&J's vaccine at a number of its facilities.[21] This pact, initiated by Bob Kadlec the previous fall, was particularly important because we were encouraging and funding companies to ramp-up their production capacity much earlier in the research and development process at a time when idle vaccine production capacity was hard to find. With that in mind, we were looking for inter-corporate collaboration—collaboration that would have been much more difficult to bring about without the DOJ's support.[22]

The DOJ's letter was a great example of the administration's "whole of government" response to the pandemic. This is a good time to note that the HHS Office of the General Counsel, led by Robert Charrow and ably staffed by Dan Barry, two outstanding lawyers, was also at our side during all of Operation Warp Speed. Whether working with the DOJ, exploring alternative uses of appropriations, or invoking the Defense Production Act, Charrow and Barry were indispensable in terms of keeping us fully within our legal limits.

BOARD MEETING DRAMA

Early on, Secretaries Esper and Azar created an OWS board, comprising representatives of the Departments of Defense and HHS and of the White House. This board, through Jared Kushner, reported directly to President Trump, and thereby minimized the typical bureaucratic decision-making processes often inhibiting speed within the federal government.

The White House Task Force, under Vice President Mike Pence at the time, was a separate governance body focused on very important, but very different priorities. It was the primary communications nexus with the governors and local leaders dealing with COVID-19 at the front lines of the pandemic every day. It was also necessarily a deliberative body, which often would take weeks at times to evaluate issues and courses of action. Dr. Deb Birx was the overall COVID response coordinator assigned to the White House Task Force.

For coordination and integration purposes, therefore, we found it only natural in May 2020, with the Operation Warp Speed board in place, to include Dr. Birx as a board member, representing input from, and communications to, the White House Task Force. Almost immediately, we found ourselves questioning this decision. Dr. Birx clearly did not understand the role of a productive board member, which in this case was to help remove barriers, contribute to the problem-solving process, and provide encouragement to a team working 24/7 to address confounding issues associated with bringing safe and effective vaccines to the public in record time.

In a well-functioning board setting, the board members play a number of important roles. They provide assistance and encouragement to their management teams, sometimes acting as mentors. They hold their management teams accountable for performance. And they are independent advocates for a variety of stakeholders, in this case, the American people. The relationships between board members and the management team should include some level of tension, given the independent, fiduciary role of the board. However, all of this should be in the spirit of properly balancing the governance function with ultimately enabling the management team to be successful.

From the beginning, the weekly Operation Warp Speed board meetings were contentious and deteriorated into strong differences of opinion between Dr. Birx and Dr. Slaoui. Birx favored the protein sub-unit vaccines manufactured by Novavax and Sanofi. Slaoui was insistent on maintaining a balanced portfolio of six vaccines across three different technology platforms. In particular, Birx was advocating an approach using Chinese hamster ovaries (CHO) employed by Genentech. The core Operation Warp Speed team would often leave these meetings completely demoralized and eventually asked if we even needed to have them.

Slaoui felt Birx was, in his words, an "overly aggressive scientist."[23] Specifically, she craved attention and control, and asserted perspectives about vaccines, but actually knew very little about vaccine development. This was the complete opposite of the ethos of collaboration and mutual respect already developed by the core Operation Warp Speed team. Indeed, in an interview conducted after he left his role as chief scientific advisor, Dr. Slaoui could not recall a single helpful idea or proposal Dr. Birx had offered as a board member.[24] Factually, if we had concentrated only on the protein sub-unit vaccines (Novavax and Sanofi), we would not have had a government-sponsored, FDA-authorized vaccine until at least the second half of 2021.

In the late summer of 2020, we held one of our weekly board meetings over at the Eisenhower Executive Office Building (EEOB), located inside the White House compound. After another bout of yelling and denigration by Dr. Birx, Slaoui told General Perna that he could no longer work with her. When Jared Kushner learned of this, he supported the Operation Warp Speed team, and the issue was resolved.[25]

Accordingly, we began to organize smaller meetings without her, outside the venue of the board, which achieved our objective of moving the team forward and lifting its spirits. All of this was a shame, as Dr. Birx had much to offer. She had a lot to contribute from a content perspective, given her coordination role on the White House Task Force. But she was too destructive from a style perspective, which, as I mentioned earlier, was perplexing, as she was very engaging and a careful listener in one-on-one interactions.

I can only speculate why she may have behaved this way. As an institution, the US Army during the 1980s, during which time she was a young officer, was not a place that had fully learned to embrace women's presence. It is likely that she earned respect by working harder, more effectively, and more strenuously defending her points of view. This seemed to play out principally in group settings during Operation Warp Speed.

One thing I can say with certainty. Deb Birx put her heart and soul into her role as the Covid-19 White House Task Force coordinator. No one on that task force worked harder than she did. She was also the one responsible for leading the effort to completely transform our pandemic response information systems, which was a great success.

OVAL OFFICE INTERACTIONS

Every few weeks, Jared would ensure we had the opportunity to brief the president. Before the first of these meetings, a small group of us, including Secretary Azar, General Perna, and Dr. Slaoui, huddled in the Roosevelt Room outside the Oval Office waiting to be called in. Each of us had tested negative for COVID during the preceding hour, which was standard protocol for anyone meeting with the president.

As we waited in the Roosevelt Room, the three among us who were nonscientists peppered Moncef with questions about the vaccine technologies and his sense about which ones would receive the first FDA green light. Moncef had been a board member of Moderna just prior to joining our Warp Speed team. He obviously knew a lot about the mRNA technology Moderna was employing. As always, Moncef's responses were measured and clear. Having successfully introduced fourteen vaccines at GSK, he was never one to "pump the sunshine." He had a realistic view of how difficult bringing a new vaccine to market could be.

It was early July, and we had been together as a team for only approximately six weeks, yet things were going well. We were narrowing the field of vaccine candidates down to fewer than ten, we were anticipating the start of two phase-III clinical trials, and we were already making progress on setting up additional manufacturing capacity. When we were called in, a few minutes after the appointed time, we were joined by the Chief of Staff Mark Meadows and Jared Kushner. Jared, as a strong proponent of the Operation Warp Speed effort, played a key role in streamlining our interactions with the president and was excited for the president to hear about our progress.

The president seemed to be in an upbeat mood. He was eager to hear how things were going and used these sessions as a means of educating himself. He demonstrated a serious level of intellectual curiosity and was deferential to both Dr. Slaoui's deep knowledge of vaccines and General Perna's four stars.

The president had a small wooden box on his desk with a red button on top that he would push when he wanted his soft drink to be refreshed. Within a minute or two of pushing the button, a steward would appear from the door to the right of the president's desk as we were facing it, and he would replace the existing glass with the new one.

After several questions about the vaccines, the president turned to therapeutics. Interestingly, he thought the ability to treat the disease, particularly for those who had been hospitalized, was going to be more important than a vaccine. His logic was both simple and compelling. He knew vaccines were only partially effective and generally given to healthy persons to prevent illness, while effective therapeutics, given to those who were already ill, would give Americans confidence that, should they contract COVID, they could be cured.

It was clear that the president obtained information from a great variety of sources—foreign leaders, pharmaceutical company chief executives, former business associates, and well-informed friends. Several of his friends and acquaintances had died from the complications of COVID, which clearly moved him. He would use this information to pose questions, but he never used it to challenge the persons sitting before him.

He was polite and deferential, but he would consistently reinforce his expectations that we would cut through any unnecessary bureaucracy and let him know if there was anything impeding our progress. He was not averse to delivering direct feedback, but more times than not, it involved a less-than-satisfactory interaction one of the Warp Speed team members had had with the media. He never challenged the team's scientific expertise, though he did note our occasional lack of clear or consistent messaging about timing of vaccine approval, estimates of doses being manufactured, or the role of the FDA.

When I asked Moncef about his impression of these meetings, he commented that he believed the president "led with intuition." He also commented that he "appreciated the fact that the president trusted us and did not micromanage the process."[26]

Was the potential timing of when we would have a successful vaccine important to the president? Of course it was. We were in the middle of a global pandemic with thousands of Americans dying each week, and he was entering the final stage of a presidential election campaign.

Would he have liked a vaccine prior to Election Day? I assume so. In his place, who wouldn't? But he never pushed the team in these meetings beyond what any reasonable executive sponsor would. He wanted safe and effective vaccines delivered to the American people as fast as possible, regardless. When he learned on November 9, six days after the election, that Pfizer had announced its extremely favorable vaccine effectiveness data, his only response to us was, "Get it out as quickly as possible. Americans are dying."

As usual, these meetings ended with his encouragement, his thanks, and his request that we let him know if we needed anything at all from him.

6

SHIPPING IT

PLANNING DISTRIBUTION AND GETTING VACCINES INTO ARMS

Think for a moment about the following mission given to General Perna and his staff in the summer of 2020: flawlessly deliver hundreds of millions of safe and effective vaccines to 300-plus million persons by the end of June 2021.

But there was a catch: With each vial of doses, the accompanying needles, syringes, and swabs must go as well. Plus, the vial must be stored in dry ice.

And there was another catch: The vaccines must ultimately be delivered to tens of thousands of inoculation centers in sixty-four different state, local, and territorial jurisdictions.[1]

Oh, and yes, no one would know until a couple of weeks beforehand which company's vaccine he would be handling, when the vaccines would be ready to ship, or what quantities would be shipped.

What the general and his staff did know in advance was that:

- some vaccines would need to be stored and transported at –80 degrees Celsius;
- some at –20 degrees;
- some would require two doses for immunity;
- some would require only one;
- for those requiring two doses, the mandatory interval between the doses could be three weeks—or four weeks;
- regardless of the interval, everyone vaccinated would need to receive the same company's vaccine both times;
- some vaccines would require small-gauge needles and syringes to administer;
- some would require larger ones.

One final catch: no one would know who had priority to receive which vaccines until the day before distribution started, which was when the CDC's Advisory Committee on Immunization Practices (ACIP) made its recommendation.

Nonetheless, General Perna promised vaccine distribution would begin within twenty-four hours of the granting of an emergency use authorization by the FDA.

There was one distribution principle the Operation Warp Speed leadership team aligned on very early: that we would not over-distribute first doses without ensuring there would always be second doses available for those who received their first doses.

Adhering to this principle was complicated by manufacturing output numbers that were changing every week and uncertainty about how many Americans in selected priority categories would come forward for their first doses, and even how many would return for their second doses. We spent most of the Thanksgiving weekend in November 2020 going through various scenarios.

Secretary Azar (remember, the self-described math geek?) developed a very sophisticated Excel spreadsheet from scratch for the team to pressure-test the impact of changes in all these different variables. This spreadsheet not only recognized the major variables but considered the fact that what happened in any given week would flow forward into the subsequent three to four weeks, depending on which vaccine it was and when second doses were due.

If all these uncertainties were not enough, distribution was complicated by philosophical differences between General Perna's team and Dr. Nancy Messonnier's team within the National Center for Immunization and Respiratory Diseases at the CDC.

Nancy Messonnier was, like so many other CDC professionals, a very capable, well-educated public servant. Reared outside of Philadelphia, she joined the CDC in 1995 after having received her undergraduate degree at the University of Pennsylvania, her medical degree at the University of Chicago, and completing her residency back at the University of Pennsylvania. In 2001, she worked as the co-leader of the anthrax response team 1 and then supported the development of a low-cost meningitis vaccine for Africa. Incidentally, she is also the former deputy attorney general Rod Rosenstein's sister.

In the early stages of the COVID-19 pandemic, she was a visible expert. Azar had known her personally for decades and had been relying on her expertise. On February 25, 2020, she was the first one to acknowledge that the disruption to everyday American life due to COVID-19 could be "severe."[2] While accurate from a scientific perspective, this message had not been completely vetted and coordinated with others and led to a significant sell-off in the global equity markets. From that point forward, at the direction of the White House and Dr. Redfield, she became less visible.

As capable as she was academically, Dr. Messonnier was not someone who inspired teamwork and collaboration. As well, she possessed a fierce belief in the capabilities of America's public health agencies and was equally entrenched in suspicion of the private sector. Additionally, like so many others in the CDC, she worked and lived in the Atlanta area, hundreds of miles from Washington, DC.

All this created tension between the Army leaders and Messonnier. Fortunately, she had a superb team beneath her in Drs. Anita Patel and Amanda Cohen. These two subordinates were in a tough position, but they were very capable and seemed to want to mitigate as much as possible the tension between Messonnier and the military leaders.

One area of tension involved funding for vaccine administration. To put this tension into perspective, basic facts are important. First, every single dose of vaccine was to be distributed *free of charge* to any location that the states and other jurisdictions designated. Second, we would deliver all the needles, syringes, swabs, face shields, and dry ice necessary to administer the vaccines *free of charge.*

On top of this, we would be reimbursing any vaccinating agency, whether private or public, approximately $25 per shot. This included reimbursing providers when they vaccinated the uninsured. As of the end of the second quarter 2021, when all Americans desiring a vaccine had access to one, over 325 million doses had been administered.[3] This represented over $8 billion in reimbursements to the vaccinators, whose costs of goods sold for the vaccine and ancillary supplies was zero.

In September 2020, we allocated $200 million to the states and jurisdictions for use in preparing to vaccinate their populations.[4] As of December 31, 2020, the states had drawn down approximately 1 percent of this $200 million.[5]

Yet Dr. Messonnier continued to lobby us for $6 *billion* more, to be distributed largely to state and jurisdictional public health entities for the

President Trump played the key role of Executive Sponsor overseeing Operation Warp Speed. The OWS core team and others meeting with the President in the Oval Office June 2020. From L to R front row Pence, Azar, Slaoui, Perna, Fauci, and Collins. Back row Birx, Hepburn, Meadows, Harrison, the author, and Kushner. Credit: The White House.

Secretary Alex Azar, the Architect of Operation Warp Speed. No other HHS Secretary in recent memory brought the wealth of relevant experience to the role. Credit: U.S. Department of Health and Human Services.

Secretary Mark Esper's unconditional support for Operation Warp Speed resulted in an unprecedented collaboration between the Departments of Defense and Health and Human Services. Credit: Secretary Mark Esper

Moncef Slaoui at the Warp Speed headquarters on the 7th Floor of the Hubert Humphrey Building in DC. He commuted to DC from Pennsylvania every week for seven months to serve the nation. Credit: Dr Moncef Slaoui.

GEN Gus Perna at a press briefing. He shied away from the media whenever he could, but he became one of our most credible spokesmen before it was over. Credit: U.S. Department of Defense.

Carlo de Notaristefani was an avid sailor, but postponed his travel plans in retirement due to COVID and joined the Operation Warp Speed Team as its senior manufacturing and supply chain advisor. Credit: Carlo de Notaristefani

"Ready, fire, aim" Bob Kadlec had the experience, know-how, foresight, and just enough irreverence to secure the hundreds of millions of needles, syringes, and vials we would need to vaccinate America before there were global supply chain constraints. Credit: U.S. Department of Health and human Services

Lieutenant General (ret) Paul Ostrowski led our interactions with the private sector partners who would near flawlessly deliver hundreds of millions of vaccine doses under stringent storage conditions. Credit: The United States Department of Defense.

Dr. Matt Hepburn, our vaccine lead had been "training for this assignment his entire career" Credit: U.S. Department of Defense

Major General Chris Sharpsten oversaw the Vaccine Operations Center (VOC), the central nervous system for vaccine distribution. Credit: The United States Department of Defense.

Dr. Peter Marks, Head of the regulatory unit within the FDA that would grant Emergency Use Authorizations for the vaccines. Credit: Chris Smith, U.S. Department of Health and Human Services.

Francis Collins developed trust-based relationships with industry leaders over a decade and he drew upon them to help make the operation a success. Credit: The United States department of Health and Human Services.

Greg D'Angelo from the White House Office of Management and Budget was instrumental in obtaining funding for OWS while Speaker Pelosi dithered in the fall of 2020 Credit: Greg D'Angelo

No one on the White House Task Force worked harder than Deb Birx, but her corrosive style detracted from her vast experience and talent. Credit: The White House.

Dr. Redfield had the difficult job of trying to lead an agency ill-prepared for such a pandemic. Credit: United States Department of Health and human Services

Dr Messionier was a dedicated and talented public servant, but would have preferred utilizing the overwhelmed state and local public health agencies instead of the more nimble, technologically-advanced, and innovative private sector. Credit: The United States Department of Health and Human Services.

The author moderating the White House Vaccine Distribution Summit, December 8, 2020. Credit: Chris Smith, U. S. Department of Health and Human Services.

The author with Col Robert "RJ" Mikesh in the Vaccine Operations Center. We could track the location of every vaccine dose every two minutes via GPS. Credit: The author.

Secretary Azar in the Vaccine Operations Center thanking the team shortly after our go-live date. Credit: United States Department of Defense

On January 12, 2021, GEN Perna bade farewell to Dr. Slaoui. The mutual respect and friendship these two developed was critical to our success and evident in this photo. Credit: The author.

purposes of vaccine administration.[6] One observer commented that Dr. Messonnier attitude was, "'Just give us the funding, and we'll make vaccine administration happen,' but she never provided any details."[7]

At wits end, we asked Dr. Messonnier and her team to itemize the specific uses of the money. We received generalities only, with one item of $1 billon for "unforeseen contingencies."[8]

That was the last straw. As good stewards of the taxpayers' dollars, this was unacceptable. When we briefed the House and Senate members every two weeks throughout the fall, we inevitably received well-placed questions (likely planted by career officials at the CDC) regarding whether the states needed more money for vaccine administration. My answer was simple: "When they come close to drawing down the first $200 million we allocated, you will be the first to know." Nonetheless, on October 16 we authorized the CDC to spend up to another $905 million in support of vaccine administration.[9]

We saw this for what it was: a "mutual admiration society" between the CDC and the country's public health agencies. Sure, these agencies had been underfunded for decades and needed to modernize. The CDC could be the sugar daddy. Given all the other budgeting factors described above, and Speaker Pelosi's refusal to pass a supplemental funding bill before the election on November 3, the core Operation Warp Speed team believed the $6 billion would be better spent advancing vaccine and therapeutic development and manufacturing. This was surely the principal source of tension.

The second source of tension involved private sector participation in vaccine administration. The Army team had to work hard to convince Dr. Messonnier that CVS and Walgreens represented the very best option to go into nursing homes and other long-term care facilities (LTCF), a task these pharmacies completed almost flawlessly just weeks into the New Year in 2021.

After returning one day from a field trip to Rhode Island to review CVS's plan of operations for completing the nursing home mission, General Perna commented that in all his years in the United

States Army, "I have never seen a more detailed, well-developed plan." Compared to most state and county public health agencies, the retail pharmacies throughout the country had better access to the cold storage required for both the Pfizer and the Moderna vaccines, they were able to hire and train thousands of vaccinators quickly, and they had developed very effective information technology systems over the years, permitting patients to make appointments online, thereby avoiding long wait times often incurred by simply showing up.

In terms of information technology, these large pharmacies also adhered to the key behavioral science principle of status quo bias. Knowing the average person has more difficulty making an appointment than cancelling one, the pharmacies required anyone seeking an initial dose of vaccine to make *the second appointment* when making the first appointment. This, hypothetically, would lead to a higher percent of patients returning for their second shots, all other things equal.

The state and county public health entities did not have the information technology systems to make this happen. They were not located in areas convenient to most Americans. They could not scale their labor forces as quickly as those in the private sector. Many of them did not even have the capability to bill third parties for their services. There was no comparison. Thus, the second source of tension.

There was much greater alignment between the Army leaders and the CDC in what the federal government's role would be and what the 64 public health jurisdictions' roles would be to "get needles in arms."

The federal government would allocate doses to the jurisdictions based on vaccine production numbers. It would also procure, organize, and ensure that kits containing all required needles, syringes, swabs, and face shields would be delivered with the vaccine doses, and it would facilitate distribution directly to the doors of the locations identified by the jurisdictions in the quantities the jurisdictions specified. Indeed, the federal government would also procure and facilitate delivery of dry ice to accompany the doses requiring special handling and cold-chain storage requirements.

In mid-September 2020, the CDC posted a sixty-to-seventy-page vaccine distribution operating playbook with detailed guidance about how this would be done and what each jurisdiction needed to do to develop very specific micro-plans complementing the federal government's overall plan."[10]

We operated off two very important principles: first, that no one knew specific jurisdictions better than those leaders closest to the ground: governors, mayors, county commissioners, and township supervisors, and second, that we never wanted the federal government's reach to exceed its grasp.

As we entered the second half of 2021, the Biden administration demonstrated clearly that it did not subscribe to this philosophy. It announced it would be sending representatives funded and directed by the federal government, knocking door-to-door around the country to "help" more Americans to get vaccinated.[11] It also insisted on establishing 100 federally sponsored mass-vaccination sites, a program it shut down after couple of months due to lack of utilization.

I would never criticize them for trying, but this new administration's authoritarian impulse to centralize all activity within the federal government was anathema to our approach. We simply did not believe we knew more about what was happening on the "corner of 5th and Vine" than local leaders and officials did. The Biden folks discovered this truth the hard way.

Our September planning document outlined, among many other items, the three separate phases of vaccine distribution.

The initial phase would be when supply was constrained and could not meet demand. We thought this would last for six to eight weeks (end of December until the middle of February). The focus during this period would be on administering vaccines to the most vulnerable and those who cared for the most vulnerable.

The second phase would be when supply essentially equaled demand, and we believed this would last another sixty to ninety days, or until approximately May 2021. During this phase, we would open distribution to more retail-like sites and broaden eligibility to a much larger percent of the population.

The third and final phase would come after May 2021 when supply would exceed demand and would have us reverting to a more normal, much less controlled vaccine distribution posture. In other words, open distribution to any qualified site and simply fulfill demand whence it came.

We asked each jurisdiction to submit its micro-plan by the middle of October, basing it on the federal government's plan and addressing six key areas: (1) use of data regarding various demographics within their jurisdictions; (2) a plan for dose allocation; (3) how they would remind citizens to return for second doses; (4) how well they were linked to our information technology systems to order doses and track those who had been vaccinated; (5) how well they were enrolling providers as vaccinators; and (6) their capacity to deal with the cold-chain storage requirements of a vaccine requiring –80 degrees Celsius storage.

Once received, we evaluated each jurisdiction's micro-plan along these lines and assigned a basic status of "red, yellow, green" to each. Where reds and yellows were most prominent, we intervened, worked with the jurisdictions, and sometimes deployed resources to the jurisdiction, if requested, until each micro-plan was sufficiently developed. The plans were ready to go by mid-to-late November.

On December 1, General Perna led what was to be one of our last planning and coordination meetings before we were to go live and begin distribution just two weeks later. The team had modeled several supply-and-demand scenarios, and each was reviewed.

We also reviewed four key tenets of the distribution plan: (1) make sure that second doses were always available; (2) a steady flow of new first doses were distributed and administered every week; (3) where possible, simplify execution to reduce risk and to absorb variability; and (4) engage in continuous learning. This last tenet was a hallmark of the distribution team. We could not possibly know how the jurisdictions, and how Americans, would react to the availability of the first vaccines, but if we could assume a continuous learning mindset, we could adapt rapidly to whatever was happening.

During this period, General Perna and his team also led a series of tabletop exercises, using various scenarios and taking specific elements of distribution and pressure-testing them for integrity. Members of the Operation Warp Speed team, principally those from the CDC, in one way or another were in continual contact with the jurisdictions during this period. We were rapidly approaching what the Army calls "snapping of the chalk line" (i.e., the start of battle), and every small facet of distribution was being examined in detail.

TIBERIUS

Mention Tiberius and scholars of ancient history think of Tiberius Caesar Augustus, Rome's second emperor (reign: AD 14 to 37). For our Operation Warp Speed team, it was the name of the information technology program we developed in partnership with Palantir Technologies, an advanced software systems developer founded by Peter Thiel of Silicon Valley fame. Our OWS team and state and local partners used it to help us with the incredibly complex challenge of tracking vaccine allocations, destinations, and inoculations. When I inquired about the name Tiberius, someone reminded me that it was Captain Kirk's middle name in the Star Trek series—thus, a clever link to the term "Warp Speed."

As we were planning our distribution strategy that summer, General Perna told his team that he wanted us "to see ourselves" all the way through the supply chain from factory to vaccine dose delivery, with vaccination numbers coming back to us from the jurisdictions. He wanted a technology-enabled system that tracked every single dose at any point in its travels. He knew that successful supply chain management required being able to identify bottlenecks and gaps early, before or as they developed, and then intervening quickly to resolve them. Very politically savvy, Perna insisted that this information system be completely auditable, in case anyone accused us of improper allocations, or diverting doses from one jurisdiction to another. In the early days of vaccine distribution, every jurisdiction wanted more doses. Many thought we were short-changing them, though we were not.

The Army team assigned two highly capable colonels to oversee the development and activation of Tiberius: Deacon Maddox and Robert "RJ" Mikesh. Tiberius's objective was to enable the entire Operation Warp Speed team, and each jurisdiction around the nation, to see instantly what quantities of which vaccines had been delivered to what locations, how many had been used, and how many were remaining. It was the "central nervous system" of Operation Warp Speed. Its output would be displayed on large screens in the Vaccine Operations Center, Warp Speed's mission control on the second floor of the HHS Humphrey Building.

Theoretically, Tiberius would permit the jurisdictions to optimize the distribution of each subsequent week's allocations of vaccines, direct citizens to places having excess supply, and keep tabs on how many folks had received first and second doses.

From a firm called OptumServe, we obtained and trained contracted information technology specialists for each of the sixty-four jurisdictions. We placed them in state and city public health offices so that there was someone to help put a finger on all forms of operational information promptly. The idea was that overwhelmed public health offices within the jurisdictions should not have to worry about how to extract information from Tiberius. Our contracted agents would do it for them.

One of Tiberius's functions was to draw upon a "data lake" of information regarding who had been vaccinated and with which vaccine. We were concerned that snowbirds in the Northeast and Northcentral US, and others like them, would receive their first doses near home just before Christmas, and then head down to South Florida after the New Year, before they had received the second doses. We didn't want them to get their second doses from the wrong manufacturer.

Hence, we wanted all the pharmacies and other vaccine administration sites to be able to call up Grandma's name and ensure she received the right second dose. This required each of the jurisdictions to permit us to draw their vaccination data into this central database. To protect individual privacy, Tiberius developers were devising an application that prevented federal officials and agencies from seeing individual names or other identifying data. Even so, some governors were slow to cooperate, particularly in the northeast. Five of the ten states with the highest COVID death rates are in the northeast,[12] making it the region most likely to benefit from the protected data-sharing we requested.

To build Tiberius, the Army colonels first visited the office of HHS's chief information officer, led capably by Jose Arrieta at first and then eventually by Perryn Ashmore later in the year. Jose and Perryn had already been working sixteen hours a day to build and perfect an epidemiological reporting system for Dr. Birx at the White House. They had very capably integrated information from throughout the Department to include test result data, hospital capacity utilization, ICU bed availability, hospital COVID admissions, mortality data by demographic, and general levels of infectivity down to the local level. The system was called HHS Protect.

We decided to utilize Palantir Technologies to take our performance to the next level. By the fall of 2020, following its initial public offering, Palantir's market capitalization had soared to over $20 billion.[13] It had already been under a contract to help develop the COVID response aspects of HHS Protect within the Department. Indeed, in the spring of 2020, it helped us set up an integrated supply chain control tower in conjunction with the nation's largest medical distribution companies such that we could track what was happening all over the country with N95 masks, surgical gloves, and gowns during a period when these were in very short supply.

Palantir was also working separately with the Department of Defense. Its expertise lay in data visualization and decision support. If we could feed Palantir data from HHS Protect and other sources, its experts could integrate, interrogate, and convert data into information and insights. Equally important, they could put it into formats instantly interpreted by even the most casual observer.

At the outset of this effort, the team General Perna assigned to lead it experienced stiff resistance from those at the CDC. While lacking any modicum of contemporary technology, the CDC still felt strongly that any data dealing with the pandemic, or our response to it, should either belong to them entirely or at least flow through them.

One observer described the CDC to me as having an abundance of "institutional pride." As an organization, it believed it had very capably responded to the H1N1 outbreak over a decade before. The same observer commented that this self-assessment of the CDC's performance during H1N1 was viewed through "rose-colored glasses" and, more important, that information technology had advanced so dramatically in the intervening years, the CDC's H1N1 legacy system was nowhere close to contemporary standards.

Attitudes at the CDC changed when it began working on the long-term care facility vaccination program. We designed this program to ensure that seniors in nursing homes and similar facilities could be vaccinated first. We knew that many of these residents were frail and vulnerable and so needed to be at the top of the priority list for vaccinations. We also knew how quickly and how deadly the virus could spread in homes for the elderly, meaning we had to put inoculators into those homes at the earliest feasible moment. So we designed a LTCF program in partnership with CVS and Walgreens.

At our request, these pharmacy chains organized and deployed mobile teams to nursing homes and long-term care facilities. The teams vaccinated residents and employees on-site. On schedule, they returned to administer the second doses. The facilities would not have to worry about supplies, tracking doses, or, in fact, any costs. Every detail was taken care of, including obtaining written authorization to vaccinate residents from their relatives when necessary.

In spring 2020, there were approximately 15,000 nursing homes in the United States, and thousands of other LTCFs.[14] Each jurisdiction would be presented with a choice: allow or not allow CVS and Walgreens to bring the federally sponsored program to their senior facilities. Once the federal program got the green light at the jurisdictional level, each LTCF within that jurisdiction could choose whether it wanted our support or not. Hospital systems owned many LTCFs, and many of these preferred to administer the shots themselves. Eventually, most others—over 90 percent of the nation's LTCFs—chose to participate in the federally sponsored program.

The CDC assigned two of its persons to sort out the logistics of the LTCF program. After two or three weeks, they were drowning in data. They had significant trouble organizing the data and verifying whether they had a complete accounting of the nation's nursing homes and long-term care facilities. This is when a couple of CDC leaders, led by Dr. Anita Patel, invited Palantir and the team of Army specialists to help.

Within a couple of days, the Palantir team resolved all the ambiguity. The system Palantir developed permitted the CDC to track daily which nursing homes were signing up, vital information, as CVS and Walgreens needed it, to match their capacity with the demand from the facilities.

Separately, and beyond the LTCF program, Tiberius soon was able to direct doses to the most underserved inner-city locations. This was through the federal retail pharmacy program. The program could tell us down to the zip code level how many persons were being vaccinated. We could target dose distribution to ensure pharmacies in hard-to-reach zip codes had adequate supply. From the very start, we were concerned about getting vaccines to communities that historically had little access to health-care services. Tiberius provided a factual basis for us to adapt and adjust distribution to do that.

Of course, as with most information technology applications, we would not know whether Tiberius worked until it worked fully. The team was racing 24/7 to get this massive project done before our go-live date. Only an extraordinary team effort among Palantir, the HHS Chief Information Office led in December by Perryn Ashmore, and the Army contingent led by Maddox and Mikesh made it happen. When we went live in mid-December and started distributing vaccine doses, Tiberius was getting information updates fed into it every two minutes through a GPS system that tracked UPS and FedEx shipments.[15]

From day one, we created and tracked performance metrics ranging from how many doses we allocated versus how many had been ordered, how many had been ordered versus how many had been shipped, how many had been shipped versus how many had been used in vaccinations, how many total doses eventually were delivered to each zip code, and how deliveries influenced vaccination rates.

Tiberius could also give us insights into our own actions, such as the impact on overall vaccination rates of adding new distribution channels (such as retail pharmacies or community health centers). The regional field leaders at the CDC used these metrics to engage in performance conversations with the jurisdictions. Tiberius became an indispensable decision support tool for the entire Operation Warp Speed team.

Tiberius is the most sophisticated vaccine distribution decision support tool the US has ever developed. I hope it will become an enduring capability of the federal government, an asset for counterattacking future pandemics.

7

DELIVERING IT

VIALS, NEEDLES, SYRINGES, AND KITS

No matter how safe and effective the vaccines might be, we could not vaccinate anyone without the requisite size and number of vials, syringes, and needles.

The vials required a special, non-breakable glass, able to handle vaccine storage at down to –80 degrees Celsius.[1] Because of the different technology platforms associated with the candidate vaccines, we found that we had to secure different sizes of syringes and different gauge needles. This task fell to Dr. Bob Kadlec. Heading the part of HHS that oversaw the Biologics and Advanced Research and

Development Authority (BARDA), he had, through BARDA, the contracting authority and financial resources to procure such essentials.

Bob Kadlec is an endlessly resourceful leader. He anticipated these needs months before anyone else. When the pandemic began, he understood that there would be a significant surge in global demand for vials, needles, and syringes, and thus, it was an imperative to move quickly to secure hundreds of millions of these for the US government.

For vials, he ultimately turned to Corning Inc. in upstate New York and SiO2 Medical Products in Auburn, Alabama. On June 1, he awarded a $204 million contract to Corning to expand its vial production capacity and a $143 million contract to SiO2 for the same purpose.[2] For syringes and needles, he engaged in much more scrounging—searching around the globe, including in China.

The vials needed to be shipped to the several "fill-finishing" plants that Carlo de Notaristefani had designated for such activity. The needles and syringes needed to be shipped to McKesson warehouses where they were "kitted."

Kitting was no simple task. The intent was to ensure that no vaccine dose destination (e.g., a nursing home, hospital, corner pharmacy) received precious vaccines possessing short shelf-lives only to be precluded from vaccinating because of a shortage of these ancillary items.

The Pfizer vaccine, for instance, shipped in minimum batches of just short of 1,000 doses. The receiving vaccination site had only seven to ten days to use all those doses.[3] We did not want doses expiring due to lack of needles and syringes.

Obtaining up to one billion needles and syringes from an already-constrained global supply chain was no mean feat.

One immediate complication was that most of the safety needles used in the United States before the pandemic were manufactured in China by companies such as Golden Well. Years earlier, our Congress passed a law designed to prevent accidental needle sticks. A care provider who accidentally stuck him- or herself with a patient's needle could contract any of many blood-borne pathogens, such as HIV/AIDS or

Hepatitis C, so this was a prudent measure. It created an enormous demand for needles with safety caps. Golden Well manufactured these types of needles. Kadlec developed a four-part strategy to ensure we met our nation's needs.

The first part of Kadlec's strategy was to contact Golden Well. When Kadlec and BARDA reached out to Golden Well in early April, however, they were told that there was no way it would be able to supply a billion needles within six months. It could only commit to a couple hundred million.[4]

For the rest of the needles, Kadlec engaged three domestically based companies (Becton-Dickinson in Nebraska, Smith's Medical in New Hampshire, and Retractable Technologies in Texas). As the second part of Kadlec's strategy, these companies expanded their manufacturing capacities to provide us with what we needed.

We encountered another unexpected complication here, too. The specialty steel needed to manufacture hypodermic needles to American standards came from South Korea. Kadlec and his team resolved this quickly. Collectively, we issued $135 million in contracts to these three companies in July 2020.[5]

The third part of Kadlec's strategy was to approach an innovative company known as ApiJect, headquartered in Stamford, Connecticut. ApiJect was developing single-dose, self-contained vial/syringe/needle combination. This device would be filled at the "fill-finish" facility in a manner similar to a vaccine vial. When it reached the vaccination site, the care provider would not have to draw the vaccine dose out of the vial because the needle was already attached to the ApiJect container. Kadlec worked with the FDA to set up a trial of this device with three different vaccines.

The last prong of the four-part strategy would only be used as a contingency. It involved seeking and obtaining a waiver from the Occupational Safety and Health Administration (OSHA), part of the Department of Labor, to use conventional, rather than safety, needles for vaccine administration. The prevention of accidental needle stick procedures had only been in place for a few years, and most experienced care providers knew how to use conventional needles safely, so this became our fallback position.

The Operation Warp Speed team had decided that we would ship all the ancillary supplies required to administer the vaccines, along with the vaccine shipments, to sites designated by the sixty-four public health jurisdictions.

To prevent vaccines from sitting idle or even expiring because of a lack of ancillary supplies, or having the wrong supplies, we asked the key packager, McKesson, to assemble hundreds of thousands of kits (essentially boxes) with the appropriately sized needles, syringes, masks, swabs, diluents, and adjuvants, and ship them to locations receiving vaccine doses in the same amounts. We even put an extra ten percent of ancillary supplies in these kits, as a backup, should a vaccinator drop a needle or a syringe. In all cases, we wanted to avoid any vaccine dose from being wasted due to lack of ancillary supplies. McKesson executed the kitting task with great skill and precision.

In the category of "no good deed goes unpunished," though, we were still criticized by the media for not including surgical gloves in these kits. Prior to assembling these kits, the OWS team checked the CDC guidance on administering vaccines, which did *not* require gloves. Still, some of the jurisdictions complained publicly.[6]

Talk about looking a gift horse in the mouth. My goodness.

In early January, we encountered yet another challenge with supplying syringes. Many of the vaccinators figured out that they could extract six, or even seven, doses of the Pfizer vaccine from vials supposedly containing only five. Given the supply-constrained situation in which we found ourselves at the time, this was an extraordinarily positive development. If we could be sure to extract six rather than five doses from a single Pfizer vial, we would overnight increase doses available by 20 percent.

The only problem was that to extract the sixth dose, the vaccinators needed what was known as "low dead volume" (LDV) syringes. Most hospitals procured these types of syringes in the normal course of business, so they were able to extract the additional dose. But we had not secured LDV syringes, and certainly had not been putting them into the kits McKesson was assembling. Retail pharmacies and other vaccination sites did not typically procure LDV syringes on their own. Thankfully, the Army Material Command team pulled another rabbit out of its hat and rapidly located, procured, and began distributing the required syringes. Like Bob Kadlec, the Army team was endlessly resourceful.

Of course, we then had to contend with Pfizer, which wanted to be *paid* for six doses per vial rather than for five. However, the FDA labelling instructions on the vial continued to indicate five doses. The FDA had granted a waiver for obtaining six doses per vial, but it had not yet changed the label, as it needed to verify that Pfizer vials would consistently produce six doses. This was eventually confirmed, and the label was changed.[7]

MAKING DISTRIBUTION HAPPEN: THE OTHER GENERALS

Much has been made of General Gus Perna's role in Operation Warp Speed, and appropriately so. But he would be the first to insist that it was a team effort. The day-to-day leaders of that team were two lesser-known generals, Lieutenant General (ret.) Paul Ostrowski and Major General Chris Sharpsten. In one way or another these two, along with General Perna, had been supporting combat operations together in the Middle East for over two decades. Collectively, they had more real-life logistics experience than virtually any team in the world. They knew logistics inside and out, they knew each other well, they knew how to lead a large-scale enterprise, and they led by example.

Paul Ostrowski is a 1985 graduate of West Point, where he excelled as a running back on the Army football team until an ACL injury, which sidelined him. As General George C. Marshall once requested during World War II, "I want an officer for a secret and dangerous mission. I want a West Point football player." In Paul Ostrowski, he would have had one straight out of central casting.

Still very fit, with a ramrod straight posture and deep blue eyes, Paul could have spent his career in Hollywood. He received a master's degree in Systems Acquisition Management at the Naval Postgraduate School and, for much of his career, he served in Special Operations Units.[8] He was approaching retirement in the summer 2020 and switched from desert camouflage to business suits during his tenure at Operation Warp Speed. Ostrowski's principal role was coordinating the many players in the private sector that would eventually form the backbone of the vaccine distribution infrastructure.

Indeed, as mentioned previously, we did not anticipate any federal employee touching a vaccine dose before its injection in an American arm. McKesson, which had a long-standing contract with the CDC for vaccine distribution, would be at the core of the private sector partners. Its role would be to receive and store all vaccines (except Pfizer's) from the manufacturers, assemble the kits comprising hundreds of millions of needles and syringes, and collaborate with FedEx and UPS to deliver the vaccines. FedEx and UPS would be the principal delivery means for all vaccines, including Pfizer's. CVS and Walgreens would be at the heart of the federal pharmacy program, eventually comprising over 40,000 retail pharmacy outlets.[9] Ostrowski had to ensure each of these parties was electronically linked into a single integrated information technology system and was feeding data into Tiberius. He had to establish all the contracts, help procure supplemental supplies and manpower as needed, and had to integrate them all to operate smoothly as a single team.

Like Ostrowski, Chris Sharpsten was also a West Point graduate, but in the class of 1988. He received an MBA from Michigan State in logistics, materials, and supply chain management. As did Ostrowski, he spent a good part of his career in special operations. Chris's son and my daughter, Hope, are both members of West Point's class of 2014, so we developed a near-instant bond.

Chris's role was focused on leading the Vaccine Operations Center. The "central nervous system" of the entire OWS distribution architecture was located deep in the second floor of the HHS's Hubert

Humphrey Building in Washington, DC. With multiple large-screen monitors covering the walls and rows of cubicles manned by a terrific group of more junior Army officers and representatives from our private-sector partners, it felt like the NASA mission control room in Houston.

The VOC was where minute-to-minute information on the status of every vaccine dose currently "in motion" came in. We knew what was leaving the factory, what was in the warehouse, what had been loaded on a UPS or FedEx plane or truck, when doses were delivered, in what quantities, to what locations, and who signed for them.

Operating twenty-four hours a day, seven days a week, the VOC was where any of us went for real-time information about what was happening that day in distribution. Despite major snowstorms, last-minute changes in vaccine production numbers, and the strong potential for human error when thousands of packages are being delivered each week to tens of thousands of locations, the VOC oversaw a success rate exceeding 99.9 percent on-time delivery to the right place without compromising very stringent storage and transport conditions.[10]

Perna, Ostrowski, and Sharpsten were also supported by a very capable bevy of other senior officers. Ted Shinkle and Matt Alexander, both colonels, handled most of General Perna's daily schedule. There were very few days during which Ted and I did not talk. Eric Shirley, another colonel, was also instrumental in the overall coordination. Lieutenant Colonel Jesse Marsalis supported most of Ostrowski's activities. I find it hard to overemphasize how committed all these officers were to the mission and the nation. Operation Warp Speed would not have been successful without them.

8

APPROVING IT

JARED'S MORNING OPERATING MEETINGS

During most of the pandemic, three major White House groups convened, if not daily, certainly multiple times a week. The White House Task Force (WHTF), led by Vice President Pence, dealt principally with interagency policy issues.

Dr. Birx led the second, less formal, "doctors' meeting." At it, she, Fauci, Redfield, and Hahn, along with others, looked closely at the epidemiological data describing the evolution of the pandemic. Their conclusions informed the policy decisions of the WHTF.

Jared Kushner chaired the third group, which was much more an operating body. It deployed resources to the COVID response areas most needing them. Out of it came several essential initiatives: the ventilator manufacturing program, ramping up COVID-19 testing capacity and access, and rebuilding the Strategic National Stockpile.

As we got into September and October, this body also laid out weekly messaging priorities. By this time, Operation Warp Speed had become a central point in the administration's overall COVID response messaging. Jared asked me to attend these sessions and provide daily updates. Several key advisors from the White House Communications Office were frequently there: Kayleigh McEnany (press secretary), Brian Morgenstern (deputy communication director/deputy press secretary), and Alyssa Farah (director of strategic communications).

Core to these meetings as well were Adam Boehler, Brad Smith, and their special assistants. Adam and Brad both came to the government after very successful stints as health-care entrepreneurs. Adam was a close friend of Jared. His first government service role was heading the Center for Medicare and Medicaid Innovation (CMMI), a unit within CMS. I was the chief of staff there at the time and got to know Adam well.

When Adam moved on to be CEO of the government's Overseas Private Investment Corporation (OPIC), we recruited Brad Smith to take his place as head of CMMI. This is where I had met Brad. All three, Jared, Adam, and Brad, were Harvard College graduates (Brad was also a Rhodes Scholar), young, successful, and brought a spirit of "nothing is too difficult" to the entire pandemic response.

Others attended as well to include Dr. Birx, Nick Butterfield from the vice president's office, John Rader (who was also close to Jared), Charlton Boyd (a special assistant to Jared), and, occasionally, Peter Navarro. Adam and Brad would typically prepare the agenda for these meetings, usually held at 8:00 or 8:30 a.m. in the Roosevelt room, and we would go through rapid but effective updates regarding the entire COVID-19 response.

THE VACCINE DISTRIBUTION SUMMIT

In mid-November, as the details of the vaccine distribution strategy were becoming clear, Jared directed us to begin planning a Vaccine Distribution Summit, kicked off by the president and intended to unveil to the outside world, through streaming technology, all the detailed planning that had gone into the vaccine roll-out program. He further asked me to work with Charlton to organize the agenda, the speakers, and where in the White House we would hold it.

After two to three weeks of intensive planning, the summit took place on December 8. We showcased the president's leadership of OWS, the crucial roles played by Secretary Azar, Dr. Slaoui, and General Perna, the exceptional leadership of several governors, both Democrat and Republican, and the enormous effort put forth by the private sector.[1] Neither Pfizer nor Moderna attended. The FDA was deeply into the process of formally evaluating their vaccines, and their presence would have raised ethical questions.

The president kicked off the day with a round of thanks to all those who made the delivery of safe and effective vaccines possible. Both Pfizer and Moderna had already reported preliminary data and had submitted their EUA applications to the FDA. It was a foregone conclusion that we were about to distribute millions of vaccines throughout the nation.

After his remarks, Mr. Trump signed an executive order, directing federal agencies to put the American people first in access to vaccines that were made in America. This order also created an interagency group to determine policy for sharing surplus US-made vaccines with allies and other countries.[2]

The stars of the afternoon were the executives from our principal private sector partners: UPS, FedEx, CVS, Walgreens, and McKesson. The executives from UPS and FedEx displayed and described the special vaccine shipping containers they had developed. Each had a GPS signaling device attached to the top, which would provide the Vaccine Operating Center in the Humphrey Building with updates every two minutes regarding the location of the container. The temperature of each container was constantly monitored, and each had a motion detector to determine whether the container was handled too roughly.

When a question came from the audience about how the shippers would handle an increase of up to a couple thousand additional vaccine containers a week during the peak holiday delivery season, UPS's executive commented that his company delivered approximately 34 million packages the day before. A couple of thousand more deliveries a week would be a rounding error.

The FedEx executive commented that most of its company's holiday deliveries went via FedEx Ground, whereas these vaccine shipments would all go by priority air. FedEx, he added, had created a separate driver training program for those who would be carrying Operation Warp Speed–sponsored vaccines. All containers would require a human-to-human drop-off and only to those locations both authorized by the state and local authorities and entered into the CDC's Vaccine Tracking System, known as VTrckS.[3]

Not surprisingly, many in the media mocked and dismissed the summit. ABC News termed it "self-congratulatory."[4] CNN headlined, "Trump makes another largely symbolic effort to combat coronavirus."[5]

Meanwhile, President-Elect Biden staged his own COVID event, announcing his health officials. As the *New York Times's* Peter Baker reported:[6]

> One president all but declared victory over the pandemic, hailing new vaccines as a "medical miracle" and congratulating himself for doing what "nobody has ever seen before." The next president declared the pandemic deadlier than ever, calling it a "mass casualty" event that is leaving "a gaping hole" in America with more misery to come.

But he added:

> Mr. Trump was correct that with his administration prodding Operation Warp Speed, the vaccine was developed faster than any has been produced before in medical history. It represents a major

> breakthrough that should change the course of the pandemic, even if not as quickly as the president has previously claimed.

At the same time, the *Wall Street Journal* reported that the day before:

> Anthony Fauci said a vaccine could diminish coronavirus as successfully as the polio vaccine did for polio, enabling workers to return to offices and restaurants in the second half of 2021.[7]

For me, it was difficult *not* to be both immensely impressed and proud of America's private sector at this point. Its participants had been innovating for decades, and we would be huge beneficiaries of this innovation. Eventually, these logistics companies would make hundreds of thousands of deliveries to tens of thousands of locations with nary a mistake. On-time deliveries to the correct location, under the correct transport conditions remained well over 99 percent for the duration of pandemic. CVS and Walgreens, to their credit, organized and vaccinated the residents of close to 15,000 of America's nursing homes essentially by the end of February or mid-March.[8] Thus, fewer than ninety days after the initial FDA vaccine authorization, the vaccines were made available to our most vulnerable citizens.

The Vaccine Distribution Summit created a great deal of confidence within our team. All the principal players saw, for the first time, how each component of logistics, distribution, and tracking had come together in a short period of time. As well, for the first time, we had laid out in public a comprehensive picture of how far the Operation Warp Speed effort had progressed. Despite subsequent protestations by members of the Biden administration and mocking in the media, the summit placed an exclamation point on what was obviously a Trump administration–led success. For all these reasons, initiating this event was a great call on Jared's part.

SCIENCE INFLUENCING POLITICS?

After the contentious meeting with Deborah Birx in the White House Situation Room on April 29, Peter Marks returned to the FDA in his role as the director of the Center for Biologics Evaluation and Research (CBER), the regulatory body that would evaluate and eventually approve or disapprove the vaccines. He pulled his team together and declared that there would be no more "business as usual."[9] Things needed to be done fundamentally differently than before. Specifically, CBER needed to accelerate its process for granting emergency use authorizations *without* compromising its standards addressing quality and safety. The only emergency use authorization ever granted for a vaccine in the United States, according to Marks, was for anthrax in 2005.[10]

In June, the FDA issued guidance for COVID-19 vaccine manufacturers. It laid out its standards and expectations for phase III (large-scale, human subject) clinical trials.[11] In short, it told the vaccine developers what the FDA would look for in granting an EUA.

With Dr. Marks deeply integrated into Francis Collins's Vaccine Operating Group within the ACTIV program, this ensured the alignment of the FDA and NIH on the vaccine guidance. Pfizer and Moderna were already conducting early-stage clinical trials, so the guidance was timely.

Among other parameters, the guidance suggested trial enrollment *not* exclude those who had already been infected with COVID-19, stressed the importance of enrolling participants most affected by COVID-19 (e.g., the elderly and minorities), and established a minimum vaccine efficacy level of 50 percent. Under safety considerations, it added that the "safety evaluation of COVID-19 vaccines ... should be no different than for other preventive vaccines for infectious diseases."[12]

The government also has a National Vaccine Injury Compensation Program, last updated in 2017. It laid out the timeline for "first symptom or manifestation of onset or of significant aggravation after vaccine administration"[13] (a great example of government-speak, isn't it?). It lists different infectious disease vaccines, the potential injury or condition covered, and then the period within which the condition needs to reveal itself to qualify for compensation under the program. The outer limit of this period for any vaccine-induced injury to qualify for compensation in this program is established at forty-two days.

Referring to the June guidance for COVID-19 vaccine development from the FDA, recommending safety evaluation be "no different than for other infectious disease vaccines," the vaccine developers naturally would have interpreted this as establishing a forty-two-day period for the revelation of vaccine-induced adverse reactions.[14]

The Trump administration was repeatedly accused of "injecting politics into science." Some said it was trying to pressure the FDA to accelerate the process and get a vaccine authorized prior to the election.[15]

Here is the truth: I attended every OWS briefing in the Oval Office and never once during these briefings did President Trump ask the team to have a vaccine prior to Election Day. Would he have liked one by then? Of course—who in his position would not have? But he never said, hinted, or implied anything along those lines.

All of this is context for what was perceived as an unusual change in guidance issued by the FDA on October 6, 2020. Just weeks before, on September 13, Albert Bourla, the chief executive officer of Pfizer, publicly stated on CBS's *Face the Nation,* "We have a good chance that we will know if the product works by the end of October."[16]

Again, on the *Today Show,* he commented that, "the company's model predicts that we will have an answer by the end of October."[17] In an open letter to his employees at about the same time he wrote, "We may know whether or not our vaccine is effective by the end of October."[18]

Thus, it was only *after* Bourla made these statements repeatedly in public that the FDA decided to issue, on October 6, its revised guidance to the original June 2020 guidance on the topic of "Development and Licensure of Vaccines to Prevent COVID-19."

Under the section labeled "Safety and Effectiveness Information," new language appeared. It read, referring to the requirements for EUA submission, "Data from Phase III studies should include a median follow-up duration of at least two months (about 60 days rather than the standard forty-two days) after completion of the full vaccination regimen to help provide adequate information to assess a vaccine's benefit-risk profile."[19]

In its briefing to the Vaccine and Related Biological Products Advisory Committee (VRBPAC) the following week on page 16 of the PowerPoint, the FDA wrote these two seemingly contradictory statements one after the other:

> "Historically, uncommon but clinically adverse events plausibly linked to vaccines (i.e., immune-mediated adverse reactions) generally have onset within 6 weeks (author's note: 42 days) following vaccination*" *Vaccine Injury Table, National Vaccine Injury Compensation Program (2017)*[20]

Then, beneath this statement on the same page:

> "Median follow-up duration of 2 months allows time for potential immune-mediated adverse reactions to be observed and evaluated"[21]

What? Even the most casual observer has to be suspicious about this. The June guidance essentially said, "Let's follow normal procedures for vaccine safety and effectiveness" referring to the injury table that had a standard of forty-two days to evaluate immune-mediated adverse reactions.

Then Pfizer, having started its phase III clinical trial at the end of July, reported it had enrolled over 25,000 participants by early September and, at the same time, asserted its own internal modelling suggested vaccine performance data may be available at the end of October (i.e., before the presidential election).[22] Only then, just two or three weeks after Bourla made these public statements, did the FDA move the goal posts with its revised guidance by imposing an additional eighteen-day requirement for EUA submission.[23]

At some level, though, while this likely discouraged Pfizer from reporting its performance data as early as it could have, it did not altogether prevent it. The independent Data Safety Monitoring Board (DSMB) for each clinical trial maintains the data on positive cases in a fashion that is blind to the manufacturer in terms of whether the positive case occurs in the placebo or the vaccinated arm of the trial.

However, the manufacturer does have insight into the *aggregate number of cases* occurring at any point in the trial. Accordingly, Bourla purportedly had insight in the number of cases aggregating in Pfizer's trial before revealing what was considered material information (i.e., potentially having an impact on the price of Pfizer's stock) for a publicly traded company.[24]

So when the FDA altered its guidance on October 6, shortly after Bourla's public statements about reporting data in late October, lengthening the time from forty-two to sixty days after the second dose for the median enrollee in the trial prior to submitting an application for an EUA, we were naturally suspicious of the underlying reason.

Pfizer wound up reporting its data publicly on November 9, just six days after the election. When it did so, the data were very favorable in terms of vaccine effectiveness. Normally data on thirty-two cases of infected enrollees could be sufficient to come to this positive conclusion. We were surprised to learn that Pfizer had accumulated outcomes of over ninety positive cases before asking for the FDA's review.[25]

When asked why he did not reveal Pfizer's data earlier, Bourla asserted that the revised guidance from the FDA precluded him from submitting his EUA application until later than originally anticipated,[26] so why not permit more time to elapse such that it could have greater confidence due to an increased number of cases? I will let the reader judge what may have been going on in this situation, but when we learned that the Biden team had information on Pfizer's data on November 8,[27] the evening before either President Trump or Secretary Azar had access to it, our suspicion could only increase.

When I spoke with Peter Marks long after this incident, though, he had a clear explanation for why the FDA did what it did. At the time, there was growing concern over vaccine hesitancy. The political barbs from both sides of the aisle may have been contributing to this, but even the moniker "Operation Warp Speed" caused some Americans to believe that the speed at which we were developing and manufacturing the vaccines would be at the expense of lesser quality.

Marks rightfully commented that developing a vaccine would have "no impact on the spread and destruction of the virus only *getting Americans vaccinated* would lead to the desired impact." He was correct. Vaccines sitting on the shelves because of vaccine hesitancy would not slow the spread of the virus. Accordingly, he and his colleagues believed the October 6 guidance was essential to shoring up vaccine confidence.

The revised guidance was a judgment call on the FDA's part. Essentially, it felt that an additional eighteen-day delay in granting an EUA during a time in which hundreds of Americans a day were dying was a reasonable trade-off if it enhanced overall vaccine confidence. I am not sure the average American citizen factors into his level of confidence the fact that sixty versus forty-two days elapsed after the median trial participant received his second dose prior to the company submitting its request for an EUA, but perhaps the medical community did.

Again, we'll let the reader determine whether or not this was "science influencing politics. But my assessment is that Peter Marks and his colleagues are honorable, hard-working career civil servants, and they likely meant well.

ANOTHER OCTOBER SURPRISE?

By his example, the president made clear to our Warp Speed team and everyone involved in the response to the coronavirus that we were not to play politics with the pandemic. Governors and other public officials were to be helped in every way possible, without regard to political party. But no governor got more special help than New York's Andrew Cuomo.

The virus hit New York particularly hard. It wasn't anyone's fault. In his recent book on the virus, *Doom: The Politics of Catastrophe*, renown historian Niall Ferguson explains that:

> The COVID-19 pandemic crisis could be understood only through the lenses of history and network science. The former provided some sense of its potential scale and likely consequences. The latter explained why the virus spread so much farther and faster in some places and some populations than in others.[28]

Regarding network science, Ferguson suggested that New York suffered from two networking curses. The first was of airline routes. New York and San Francisco were the only two US cities that received direct flights from Wuhan, nineteen between them from December 1, 2019, to January 23, 2020. The second was the layout of the city itself, "from stuffy buses to senicidal old folks' homes." He might have added, not just buses but subways, too, and high-rise apartment houses, with elevators that became vertical mini subways, in which much of its population lived.

In March, the overwhelmed governor appealed to the president[29] who, on March 18,[30] ordered the Navy hospital ship *USNS Comfort* to New York. It arrived on March 30.[31] Not set up for the specific needs of the virus, the ship was intended, as the *New York Times* reported the day after it docked, "to take patients with other medical problems to relieve New York hospitals overrun by virus patients."[32] Yet Governor Cuomo seems never to have pushed his health officials to develop a plan of use that might have given some measure of relief to hospitals, and the *Comfort* remained empty. Instead, on March 25 Mr. Cuomo issued his notorious order barring nursing homes from refusing transfers of COVID patients from those pressured hospitals to nursing homes.[33]

Continuing his effort to address New York's hospital-bed shortage, in April, again in coordination with the governor, the president ordered the Army Corps of Engineers to outfit Manhattan's convention facility, the Javits Center, as a field hospital.[34] But, again, New York officials developed no plan of use with the military, and instead of being used to relieve the hospital overcrowding by taking non-COVID patients, beds in the center, like those on the *Comfort*, stayed empty. Ultimately, military health personnel fanned out through the city to help wherever hospital staff-shortages were severe. [35]

Despite all of the president's efforts on behalf of New York, in late October, with two vaccines seeking FDA emergency use authorizations and the willingness of people to be vaccinated already recognized as a major concern, the governor decided to join the so-called experts, the media, Joe Biden, and so many others over the course of the year. Just days before the election, he played politics with the health of New Yorkers and anyone hearing him around the country. In a nationally broadcast interview with the network's George Stephanopoulos:

> Governor Cuomo said that he's not "that confident" in the [FDA] approval process [under President Trump].
>
> "My opinion doesn't matter, but I don't believe the American people are that confident. You are going to say to the American people now, 'Here's a vaccine, it was new, it was done quickly, but trust this federal administration, their health administration that it's safe, and we're not sure of the consequences,' I think it's going to be a very skeptical American public about taking the vaccine, and they should be," Cuomo said.
>
> Stephanopoulos asked Governor Cuomo what it would take for him to be convinced that it's safe, effective and should be distributed.
>
> "What I said I'm going to do in New York is we're going to put together our own group of doctors and medical experts to review the vaccine and the efficacy and the protocol, and if they say it's safe, I'll go to the people of New York and I will say it's safe with that credibility," he said. "But I believe, all across the country, you are going to need someone other than this FDA and this CDC saying it's safe."

As we approached the summer of 2021, Governor Cuomo was perplexed that so many New Yorkers refused vaccination. He began talking about coercive measures to counter the vaccine hesitancy on which he himself had started the ball rolling months before.

A VISIT FROM VICE PRESIDENT PENCE

Vice President Mike Pence spent most of the year 2020 leading the White House Coronavirus Task Force (WHTF). As a former governor, Pence possessed the experience, knowledge, and capabilities for this role: a deep understanding of what happens at the state level, a sense of empathy for the role of governors, how the public health system works, and the soft touch of a seasoned political leader.

A former congressman, he also understood how to manage the Hill and the dynamics associated with getting bills passed and obtaining the financial support needed in a national emergency. The vice president was often prone to be, as the saying goes, "lavish in his praise and hearty in his approbation." He was fiercely loyal to his boss, the president, and would alter his cheerful demeanor whenever anyone was even implicitly casting aspersions on Mr. Trump.

He had four very difficult tasks in this role, and he performed them admirably. First, he had to coordinate what was a "whole of government" response across cabinet departments and their agencies. As the pandemic evolved, these agencies principally included the Federal Emergency Management Agency (FEMA), led by the very capable New Englander Pete Gaynor, and located within the Department of Homeland Security, and the various elements of HHS, including FDA, CDC, and NIH. Early on, and intermittently, the COVID response also needed to draw upon the Departments of State, Transportation, Labor, and Treasury. Vice President Pence had both the demeanor and experience to align all these various parts of the federal government.

Second, Pence had to lead the communications with the governors primarily through what ended up being approximately forty weekly calls, but also through very many one-on-one phone calls and visits to their states.

Third, he had to lead the task force itself, comprising cabinet secretaries, White House advisors, and medical experts. This included not only coordinating their resources but coordinating the federal government's outgoing messaging to the media and the American people.

Fourth, he had to keep President Trump abreast of all COVID-19 developments.

As discussed previously, there was overlap between those serving on the White House Task Force and those serving on the Operation Warp Speed board. These included Secretary Azar, Dr. Fauci, Dr. Birx, Dr. Redfield, and Jared Kushner.

So the White House Task Force remained informed of the progress we were making, how to message certain milestones, and could convey progress and updates on vaccines and therapeutics to the governors on the weekly calls. On several occasions, I went over and briefed the task force myself. Nonetheless, we intentionally separated the decision-making and governance roles of the White House Task Force from those of the Operation Warp Speed board, ensuring we went straight to the president, through Jared, for key Warp Speed decisions. Operation Warp Speed was designed with speed in mind, and the White House Task Force was necessarily more of a deliberative body.

As we got closer to the point of vaccine distribution, however, the vice president asked if he could visit us at the HHS offices to discuss the anticipated vaccine allocation methodology and how this aligned with prioritization of who should be offered the vaccine first. Tension had been growing for several weeks among three parties.

There was Dr. Redfield, director of the CDC, who knew he had to deal with the Advisory Committee on Immunization Practices (ACIP), an independent body whose members advised the CDC on who should be prioritized for vaccination once a vaccine was granted an EUA.

There was Dr. Birx, who reviewed daily the COVID infection and fatality numbers and understood in great detail what demographic and underlying clinical characteristics resulted in the most severe cases.

Then there were Generals Perna and Ostrowski, who had to deal with the "physics" of getting millions of vaccines out each week and were in the crosshairs of the jurisdictions demanding more information for planning purposes.

The various positions had hardened over the several weeks, with

Dr. Birx arguing for an allocation based on numbers of elderly and potentially minorities; Dr. Redfield in general agreeing with this, but also remaining deferential to what the ACIP may recommend; and Generals Perna and Ostrowski arguing for simplicity, and therefore a straightforward per capita allocation (i.e., jurisdictions would receive a share of vaccines each week proportional to their populations as a percent of the total United States population).

We ran through many different scenarios for each jurisdiction to include numbers of front-line health-care workers, those over sixty-five years of age, and the like. Indeed, the differences in these populations among jurisdictions would have significantly altered allocation amounts.

But there were other considerations, too, such as how would we treat snowbirds who traveled from New York State or Pennsylvania to Florida in early 2021. What if some states legitimately thought they should vaccinate teachers first? How about states with truly essential workers, such as meatpackers or public transportation operators?

And, of course, one of the most significant items was how would we deal with large cities whose employee bases commuted from different jurisdictions. Would health-care workers commuting from New Jersey to work at Columbia Presbyterian Hospital in northern Manhattan be entitled to use New York City's vaccines, or would they need to get vaccinated off-duty in New Jersey? If we used underlying health conditions as a factor, how would we get this information on 330 million Americans?

Vice President Pence was drawn into this situation in the late fall of 2020 most likely by Dr. Birx. Although the Vice President, as the leading communicator with the nation's governors during the pandemic, certainly had a legitimate reason to be independently interested in this topic. As one can imagine, planning a visit from the vice president of the United States is no simple task. The Secret Service arrives the day before, hallways are blocked, metal-detecting wands are deployed, and points of egress from various rooms are studied. As well, the "strap hangers" (those not relevant to the discussion but wanting to be seen with the vice president) come out of the woodwork. Meanwhile, name cards and seating charts are drafted, reviewed, and finalized, and a precise run of show (e.g., the vice president arrives downstairs at 12:26 p.m., enters elevator at 12:28 p.m., meets and greets from 12:30 to 12:37 p.m., meeting called to order at 12:41 p.m., etc.) is created.

This day, November 19, however, the main character was not going to be the vice president, rather it would be General Gus Perna. The vice president's role would be to pose penetrating questions about the distribution scheme, its rationale, risks, contingencies, and alternatives. He was well prepared.

About seven minutes into the meeting, though, it became clear why Gus Perna had risen to be a four-star general, overseeing the US Army's Material Command. He had command of every detail, described the reasoning for why we needed to follow a set of tried-and-true distribution principles, articulated the alternatives we had considered and why he thought they were inferior to the primary course of action, and asserted enthusiastic support for his team's chosen course of action.

Everyone in the room was speechless, including Drs. Birx and Redfield. With the exception of General Perna occasionally referring to the vice president as "Mr. Secretary," it was an impressively flawless performance. The vice president, gracious as usual, was "lavish in his praise," and appeared appropriately impressed with General Perna after having all of his questions answered. This ended the debate on vaccine allocation methodology. A week later, we learned that Dr. Birx had, in violation of her own guidance, spent much of Thanksgiving weekend with three generations of her family. Her influence and credibility with the Operation Warp Speed team collapsed.

SUPPORTING VACCINE DIPLOMACY

When we hosted the Vaccine Distribution Summit in the South Court Auditorium of the White House on December 8, we put on display all the innovative approaches our partners such as McKesson, UPS, FedEx, Walgreens, and CVS had undertaken to ensure the reliable delivery and administration of hundreds of millions of vaccine doses.

This was also the event at which President Trump issued Executive Order 13962, "Ensuring Access to United States Government COVID-19 Vaccines." While criticized by the media for putting Americans first,[36] the executive order was equally focused on conditions and procedures for delivering safe and effective vaccines to the rest of the world.

Section Four of the executive order was titled "International Access to United States Government COVID-19 Vaccines" and said:

> After determining that there exists a sufficient supply of COVID-19 doses for all Americans who choose to be vaccinated, as required by section 3(b) of this order, the Secretary of Health and Human Services and the Secretary of State, in coordination with the Administrator of the United States Agency for International Development (USAID), the Chief Executive Officer of the United States International Development Finance Corporation, the chairman and president of the Export-Import Bank of the United States, and the heads of other agencies, shall facilitate international access to United States Government COVID-19 Vaccines for allies, partners, and others, as appropriate and consistent with applicable law.[37]

The executive order went on to require the National Security Council to develop this plan within thirty days.

This was a particularly important international topic as China and Russia were already actively, and somewhat promiscuously, distributing their vaccines around the world. Sinovac, a Chinese vaccine production company, had a vaccine that the World Health Organization (WHO) declared effective at the 50.4 percent level.[38]

The US FDA's minimum standard for EUA approval of a COVID-19 vaccine was 50 percent, and, of course, all of our approved vaccines exceeded this standard by a wide margin. As one can imagine, the demand for Pfizer, Moderna, AstraZeneca, and Johnson & Johnson vaccines globally far exceeded that for Sinovac's.

Within HHS resides a little-recognized organization known as the

Office of Global Affairs (OGA). It houses about seventy persons with previous experience typically in either the CDC, FDA, or NIH. It also has seven international attachés stationed in Switzerland, Mexico, Brazil, China, India, Kenya, and South Africa. Its principal mission is to engage in global health policy and diplomacy with the World Health Organization as its primary focus. It interacts with Health Ministries around the world as well[39] and provides advice and counsel to the HHS secretary.

In 2020, OGA was led by Garrett Grigsby, a seasoned, competent executive with prior experience at USAID and the Senate Foreign Relations Committee. When COVID-19 broke out in January of 2020, Garrett and his team's visibility within the department grew instantly and significantly.

His team tried to gain intelligence from China early on with no success. More important, Garrett set up what were to become twenty-two calls among the G7 health ministers, led by Secretary Azar, approximately one every other week during 2020. These calls were to exchange information about the pandemic, to coordinate responses, and to share best practices. Given Japan's involvement in the calls twelve time zones away, we always held them early in the morning, East Coast time.

In July, approximately six weeks after the Operation Warp Speed kickoff in the Rose Garden, Secretary Azar was confident enough of its potential success that he directed Grigsby to begin developing a plan that he eventually titled "Global Distribution of Excess Vaccines."[40]

Azar anticipated that once we had safe and effective vaccines, "the whole world will be knocking at our door."[41] Over the subsequent several weeks, Garrett engaged Brian Cavanaugh at the National Security Council, who facilitated the involvement of members of the State Department, Department of Defense, and the Development Finance Corporation (DFC), formerly called OPIC, led by Adam Boehler.

The plan this group eventually developed for distributing surplus vaccines divided the world's countries into four categories. First were our strategic allies, such as Israel or Taiwan. Second were those countries collaborating with us on vaccine clinical trials, such as South Africa and Brazil. Third were those generally indigent countries that we supported with foreign assistance and USAID aid during non-pandemic times. This group included countries that would have trouble getting vaccines any other way. Last would be all other countries, excluding China and Russia.[42]

Collectively, these four categories comprised over 100 countries. Given the complexity of negotiating so many agreements, the plan was to use the Global Alliance for Vaccines and Immunization (GAVI) as an intermediary. GAVI had been created originally to help fight HIV/AIDS and then evolved to malaria and other communicable diseases. It had already worked out the liability and logistics issues associated with distributing vaccines and therapeutics to remote reaches of the world. It was a natural partner.

So by the time the executive order was issued on December 8, the joint team led by the Office of Global Affairs and the National Security Council had a plan in place to take care of the rest of the world. When, in 2021, the United States entered phase three of the CDC's distribution plan issued the prior September, the supply of US-made vaccines was beginning to exceed domestic demand, and the Biden administration began activating these international distribution plans, very much as we laid them out.

SUCCESS: MODERNA AND PFIZER GRANTED EMERGENCY USE AUTHORIZATIONS

In December 2020, as we approached the moment when FDA would grant emergency use authorizations or not, throughout the Operation Warp Speed team, the excitement and suspense were palpable.

By the third week of December, after Pfizer had received its emergency use authorization a couple of days earlier, the Vaccine and Related Biological Products Advisory Committee (VRBPAC) of the FDA was meeting for the second time in two weeks. Composed of external experts, the group reviewed all clinical trial data and FDA's analyses and then collectively advised the FDA on whether to proceed, in this case with an emergency use authorization for the Moderna vaccine. Its meetings are public and video-streamed. They can last five or six hours or more, so one needs to have a lot of patience.

It was late in the afternoon that day, and the sun was shining in Moncef Slaoui's seventh-floor office in the Humphrey Building. As I walked in, I saw he was the only one there. He was watching the VRBPAC meeting on a large monitor mounted on his office wall.

"How's the meeting going?" I asked. He thought very well, but he was most interested in the voting, which was going to begin presently. As a former board member at Moderna, Moncef had an intense interest in the outcome. More important, he knew the Moderna vaccine was the first one the Operation Warp Speed team had ushered through every step of research, development, testing, and manufacturing. This was our "baby."

The Pfizer vaccine, approved days before, did not have the same emotional impact on our team. It wasn't even really a Pfizer vaccine. It was distributed by Pfizer, but it was actually developed by BioNTech, a small company in Germany. While heavily supported by Operation Warp Speed in many ways, including a $2 billion advanced purchase order for 100 million doses, Pfizer consistently chose to operate at arm's length.[43] So we did not feel nearly the personal ownership of Pfizer's success as we did of Moderna's.

Moderna became a partner with the government in early 2020, even prior to the official formation of Operation Warp Speed, and developed its vaccine in conjunction with and investment from the NIH. We then helped it expand manufacturing capacity and set up its clinical trial sites. We guaranteed purchase of its output. We had also granted it "Defense Production Act" privileges, giving it a priority rating for raw materials and other supplies.

Then, too, the Moderna vaccine was far easier and less costly to distribute. It did not require the minus 80-degree Celsius storage and transport requirements of the Pfizer vaccine, and it could be shipped in batches of 100 doses as opposed to Pfizer's batches of 975.[44]

As the voting began, Moncef was clear that he was hoping for unanimous support, meaning all twenty-one members would vote to recommend an EUA. We were both disappointed to learn that the outcome was twenty "yeas" and one abstention. How could someone not support one of the safest and most effective vaccines ever developed? Nonetheless, Moncef and the entire OWS team nearby were delighted. We now had two safe and effective vaccines, and 2020 was not over. More important, Moderna had already manufactured approximately 13 million doses that were ready to ship throughout the country.[45]

As I walked into General Perna's office, I remembered a line in David McCollough's *Path Between the Seas.* McCullough was describing the construction of the Panama Canal, but I applied it to our adventure. "General Perna," I said, "Operation Warp Speed is no longer a matter of scientific discovery. It is now one of physical magnitude." He knew exactly what I meant. From here on in, the challenge would be vaccine distribution and administration. This was only days before Christmas 2020. Would timing complicate the challenge?

9

SHOWTIME

THE ACIP AND THE CDC

The Advisory Committee on Immunization Practices (ACIP) is similar to the VRBPAC's role with the FDA. It is an independent body that advises the CDC on who among those eligible to receive vaccinations should receive priority. It was established by the surgeon general in 1964, and its recommendations quickly became the basis for which inoculations the federal government and the private health insurance sector would reimburse health-care providers for administering. It typically comprises fifteen members whose expertise ranges from public health to laboratory vaccine research, to "social and community aspects of immunization programs."

The ACIP in this case was to meet immediately on the heels of the FDA granting an emergency use authorization (EUA) for each vaccine candidate. Its task was to consider the EUA's parameters (for instance, in the case of Pfizer, the EUA did not extend it to children under sixteen years old because the clinical trial did not include anyone beneath this age).

As with many other aspects of the pandemic response, however, differences of opinion were beginning to surface in the weeks preceding the first anticipated EUA and subsequent ACIP meeting date.

Dr. Bob Redfield, as described earlier, is not one who embraces confrontation. He already had a keen sense for where the ACIP's recommendations would land, and this would be in favor of prioritizing front-line health-care workers first to receive vaccinations.

The ACIP had already met earlier in the fall in a preliminary session and had somewhat revealed its hand. As director of the CDC, Dr. Redfield had the authority to overrule the ACIP's recommendations. He would not consider this lightly, however, as he had been a longstanding member of the public health community. As well, the media would certainly characterize any modifications to this "independent body's" recommendations as somehow politically motivated.

Enter Deborah Birx, the White House Task Force COVID-19 coordinator. She had been studying the case fatality rates for several months and understood clearly that those with certain demographic or underlying health condition characteristics could be twenty to thirty times more susceptible to clinical complications, hospitalization, and death from COVID.

She also knew that, at that point in time, despite the heroic efforts to care for COVID-19 patients, only approximately 230,000 out of about 21 million (1%) US health-care workers had even tested positive for the virus. In other words, with all of their personal protective equipment (PPE), meticulous operating procedures, and general sensitivity to infection control, health-care workers were not as vulnerable to infection as many thought.

She was appropriately advocating for ensuring seniors in nursing homes (the most vulnerable among the vulnerable, statistically) to occupy the top spot in terms of vaccination priority. On a per capita basis, nursing homes had experienced some of the highest fatality rates in the country.[1]

Dr. Redfield, favoring the ACIP's preference for front-line health-care workers going first, also introduced some sound logic to the argument: a ninety-year-old in a nursing home had a much higher probability of dying from any cause within six months of receiving a vaccine than most front-line health-care workers did, completely independent of the vaccine itself.

Under emergency use authorization standards, the FDA would have to evaluate any fatality within this timeframe as potentially being associated with the vaccine. Having the FDA investigate a large number of post-vaccination fatalities, even among ninety-year-olds, could lead to an unnecessary decline in what was already a shaky state of vaccine confidence. So Dr. Redfield had strong support for his position to give priority to front-line health-care workers.

Secretary Azar had been carefully absorbing both Dr. Redfield's and Dr. Birx's logic and assertions during Operation Warp Speed board meetings. He asked Dr. Redfield to ensure we scheduled a time to meet as a small group immediately after the ACIP issued its recommendations but before he certified these recommendations, as the CDC director was required to do.

Azar was hoping for a collaborative discussion among several key experts and further believed that such a meeting would help Redfield deal with any potential criticism should the group decide to modify the ACIP's recommendations. Redfield would be able to claim accurately that a group of expert colleagues met and believed any modification was necessary.

Shortly after the ACIP met on the day after Pfizer received its emergency use authorization, however, its recommendations were published in the CDC's Mortality and Morbidity Weekly Report (MMWR).[2] We were surprised, to say the least, to be reading about the recommendations before we had met as a group to discuss them as Azar had requested.

Had someone within the CDC dealing with the ACIP mistakenly published the recommendations without Dr. Redfield's knowledge or approval? No. What we learned is that Dr. Redfield certified the ACIP's recommendations in writing before the publication.

One could characterize this as insubordination at some level, but Dr. Redfield was in a very difficult position. He is a warmhearted professional, has keen insights into public health challenges, but he is not a gifted debater. He probably understood that his argument in support of front-line health-care workers would not have carried the day with Dr. Birx and all her facts on the other side of the argument. So he did what he thought was best in the long run. As the saying goes, "It is sometimes easier to beg for forgiveness than to ask permission."

At its conclusion, the ACIP's recommendations really did not matter that much. Each jurisdiction had the authority to prioritize its citizens for vaccination however it wished. For instance, some jurisdictions elevated teachers into higher categories. Others, such as West Virginia, put those in nursing homes at the top.[3] But it does represent another example of the tension, differences of opinion, and how decisions were actually made during the very intense period of the pandemic response.

DAY 1 IN THE VACCINE OPERATING CENTER (VOC)

The Vaccine Operating Center became the "central nervous system" for all logistics related to vaccine storage and distribution. Large-screen monitors displayed virtually any piece of information about the disposition of millions of vaccines.

This information included which vaccine doses were being released from inspection, which had been allocated to whom that week, which had been ordered from the allocation, where the orders were destined, an ability to track their location in two-minute intervals, and, finally, who had signed for them at the destination.

Representatives from McKesson, FedEx, and UPS were present in the VOC to address any real-time issues with their respective companies during the storage and distribution effort. The center was staffed by a dozen or so officers at any one time from several branches of the service, ranging from captains to full colonels. Major General Chris Sharpsten was at the helm. There were four or five rows of cubicles, each with a monitor of its own, and every participant had an assigned role.

In one of the offices off the main room was Col. Robert J "RJ" Mikesh, an outgoing and energetic officer who was constantly mining data from Tiberius. Early on, one of the key metrics captured how long it took the jurisdictions to report their respective vaccination numbers. RJ knew this figure down to the hour, and in the first couple of weeks after "D-Day," as we called the first day of vaccine shipments, the average lag in reporting was ninety to ninety-six hours.[4] So immediately a gap existed between what was shipped and what had been reported as vaccinated.

Major Doug Meyer was another prominent figure in the VOC, and he quickly became my go-to guy for information. Secretary Azar expected me to stay abreast of all distribution developments, as well as its current status, so spending time in the VOC each day was essential, and the officers there could not have been more helpful. Doug even started sending me unsolicited information, anticipating what I might need to know.

Day 1 in the VOC was exciting. It was mid-December, the day after the FDA granted Pfizer its EUA. General Perna had been asserting for months that the first vaccine shipments would go out within twenty-four-hours of the time a manufacturer received its emergency use authorization, and, sure enough, this is exactly what happened.[5]

As General Perna commented several times, the planning phase was over; now it was "all about physics": getting millions of vaccines to the right places in the right quantities, while maintaining the appropriate storage and transport conditions. Every container of vaccines was continuously monitored for temperature. If there was a temperature "excursion" (meaning a deviation), we would know about it right away.

Curiously, the Pfizer vaccines had the most frequent temperature excursions. Their temperatures were becoming even *cooler* during shipment than the –80-degree Celsius requirement. The Pfizer people told us that this would not spoil the vaccine in any way, so all these vaccines were eventually used. Vaccines needed to be shipped from Pfizer's plant in Kalamazoo, Michigan, to the UPS and FedEx staging sites in Kentucky, and from there they would be shipped all over the country.

The atmosphere was energized by the knowledge that, after a half-year of planning, training, and piloting, it was time to go live. Everything had been tested and retested several times, we had completed many tabletop exercises under General Perna's leadership, and there was a great deal of confidence about successful execution.

The first day went flawlessly. I mentioned half-jokingly to Chris Sharpsten afterward that we should go get a keg of beer for the troops to celebrate. From my own days in the service, I know the troops would have appreciated this, and there was great cause for celebration. In the end, though, boisterous celebration seemed inappropriate. Hundreds of Americans were dying each day from COVID-19. We settled for the quiet satisfaction successful execution gave us.

The Vaccine Operations Center continued to act as the central nervous system of the Warp Speed entire enterprise. It was an indispensable asset in a rapidly evolving environment in which real-time information was vital to success. The military leaders we had did an exceptional job. They contributed brilliantly and nobly to our success.

THE FIRST WEEKS OF DISTRIBUTION: A MEDIA FRENZY

Recall that the first two emergency use authorizations were granted to Pfizer and Moderna on December 11 and December 16, respectively.

But while vaccine *distribution* was going flawlessly during the first few weeks, vaccine *administration* (in other words, injection) numbers were foundering. We suspected that good deal of this reflected a lag in reporting. A four-day lag in the first two weeks[6] represents about 25 percent of the elapsed time and could easily create a few million-dose gap between what we had distributed and what was reported to have been vaccinated.

We were surprised to learn, however, that much of this gap was because many front-line health-care workers (estimated at 30%), and many nursing home employees (reported to be closer to 50%), were declining to get vaccinated.[7] After all, many of them were in close contact with COVID-19 infected patients daily.

We had seen signs of public doubts about a vaccine. In early December, Dr. Fauci had told a *Wall Street Journal* conference:

> There are a substantial proportion of people who do think this is not real, that it's fake news, or it's a hoax. This is extraordinary. I've never seen this before," he said. Dr. Fauci added that he will convey the following to President-elect Joe Biden's administration: "We have all got to be on the same page telling the American public we have to pull together. That, to me, is the most important thing."[8]

This hesitancy demonstrated by two top priority groups put us in a predicament. We had meticulously planned shipments to these groups, anticipating that they would be eager to participate. Hospitals were the predominant destination for our early shipments, but the requirement for Pfizer vaccines to be shipped and stored at –80 degrees Celsius, in batches of approximately 975 doses, and then to be used within seven days or so meant that once these boxes reached their initial destination, they could not simply be re-packed and shipped elsewhere if not all doses were consumed.

The barrage of media criticism pounding us every day by early January was intense. The media and the incoming Biden administration were clearly trying to characterize the vaccination effort as a failure, and the reason it was failing was because the Trump administration had "no plan."[9]

The truth, of course, was that there were actually sixty-five plans: one overarching master plan composed by the CDC, and one microplan from each from the sixty-four public-health jurisdictions. Indeed, an immense amount of detailed planning had taken place by the federal government, the local jurisdictions, and our private-sector partners. The incoming administration's comments were an insult to hundreds of career federal employees, every governor, and many large-city mayors comprising the sixty-four health jurisdictions, and some of the most capable, iconic corporations in the world.

Anyone who conducts planning as a profession, however, understands that one cannot plan for every possible contingency and eventuality, particularly as they relate to human behavior. Indeed, many of the best planners in corporate America refer to the optimal sequence of planning and execution as "design it, try it, fix it, scale it." This point is that many uncertainties have only one path toward clarity and resolution, and that path is *time*.

Until one begins the *execution* of a plan, there is absolutely no way to understand how various participants and stakeholders will react. The critical task in these situations is to have one's antennae close to the action, learn what is happening, and adapt quickly. Secretary Azar wanted to convene an in-depth strategy session with the Operation Warp Speed distribution team principals for exactly this purpose, so we headed out to Camp David for a half-day session.

THE CAMP DAVID SUMMIT AND RAPID ADAPTATION

For several weeks, the senior HHS team had been planning a trip to Camp David. As the end of our administration approached, we wanted to assess what we had done well and what we could have done differently.

The date was set for Thursday, January 7. While the events at the Capitol the day before startled us, they were irrelevant to the work we had before us, which was to get as many Americans vaccinated as possible.

Given the shortfalls that health departments around the nation were facing in receptiveness to vaccination, we decided to alter the purpose of our meeting and spend half the day delving into the actual reasons for the shortfall and how to get back on track. Of course, when word leaked out that we were conducting this "separate meeting," the media framed it as a sign of breakdown when the real story was repair.[10]

Camp David is about an hour and fifteen-minute drive from downtown DC, located in the serenity of the Catoctin Mountains of northern Maryland. Security there is tight, to say the least. One cannot simply drive up to the front gate and be admitted. Several miles before the entrance is an obscure, unlabeled, parking lot. A bus from the Camp arrives, and several heavily armed marines hop off to identify, brief, and "wand" each visitor. All of us had submitted names and social security numbers in advance for what would certainly be background checks.

The Camp itself is a collection of buildings and cottages from different eras, dating back decades. We were let off at what looked like a relatively modern structure named Laurel, a conference center with highly secure "situation rooms" and a working office for the president. The staff there were all trained hospitality professionals eager to ensure we had a pleasant experience. We were not disappointed. We received ample amounts of coffee, snacks, and water, all of which were classified as "private expenses," and for which our credit cards were graciously accepted.

After Secretary Azar's brief introductory remarks, we turned to how we could improve the rate at which vaccine doses were getting into arms. At the time, we had shipped millions more doses than had been reported injected. The diagnosis of the key issues became clear: The ACIP's recommendations to prioritize front-line health-care workers first, principally by shipping large numbers of doses to hospitals, was limiting the reach and impact of the roll-out.

Also, several jurisdictions had agreed very late to have CVS and Walgreens handle their nursing home vaccinations. In each of these jurisdictions, every time a pharmacy received a late green light, it triggered a two- to three-week ramp-up period. The pharmacy companies had to hire, train, and deploy the staff necessary to get the job done. Some jurisdictions were doing great, while others had fallen far behind. We needed to help them catch up.

Finally, the jurisdictions were very likely vaccinating more persons than they were reporting to have vaccinated but were submitting their reports late.

The media and others, who were clueless about logistics and the vagaries of vaccine manufacturing, were also critical of us holding back millions of second doses in the warehouses.[11] Why had we shipped so many more doses than were being used, they asked, even as they also asked, why we weren't shipping more doses.

There were two important reasons for holding back doses. The first I addressed earlier. We had made a commitment that anyone getting a first dose would have access to a second dose. Any early period of manufacturing and shipping is inevitably unstable. To be sure we could keep the promise, we needed to keep the second doses on hand.

There was a second reason, though. Pfizer had pledged in September that it would likely deliver 50 million doses to us before year's end. Our contract with Pfizer committed them to delivering 20 million doses in November and 20 million doses in December. The 50 million would have exceeded our contractual expectations.

As the autumn wore on, however, Pfizer began reducing the numbers of doses we could expect to receive. When November came, it failed to deliver *any* doses at all. Still, in early December, Pfizer management thought it could still get us 22 million before year's end.[12] They did not. We received only 18 million.

So from the first week in December to the end of December, Pfizer's estimate dropped by close to 20 percent.[13] Needless to say, in those early weeks, when it came to Pfizer's manufacturing process, we had little confidence at all.

By the time of our meeting at Camp David on January 7, however, we were approaching the fourth week of Pfizer's dose distribution, and the third week of Moderna's. The manufacturing and delivery numbers were stabilizing. The second doses for the initial inoculations weeks before were ready to go out. These very positive developments led us to decide that, starting the following week, we would no longer hold back second doses.

We made four other important decisions that morning. First, we would recommend that jurisdictions expand the number of vaccine distribution destinations to include retail pharmacies. Working with our state and local partners, we had already registered approximately 40,000 retail pharmacy locations, which had done the hiring and training of inoculators, so these sites could be turned on instantaneously.

Second, we recommended that all jurisdictions expand eligibility for vaccination to anyone over sixty-five years of age. This, we felt, would still ensure we were focusing on the most vulnerable, while better balancing demand with supply.

The third decision was the most controversial. Members of the Biden Administration reversed it when they took office. To balance supply with demand, we believed that the state and local health agencies that had not yet used the equivalent of the previous week's allocation should forfeit their subsequent week's allocations to jurisdictions that were fully using what we were giving them.

The fourth and final decision was part and parcel of the third. We would begin publicly posting vaccine administration performance, jurisdiction by jurisdiction. The numerator would be the number of vaccinations. The denominator would be the number of doses delivered.

The following Tuesday, January 12, Secretary Azar and Dr. Redfield hosted a press conference at HHS to announce these changes.[14] To Dr. Redfield's credit, he was willing to confront the ACIP's initially narrow recommendations and announce that jurisdictions should expand both access and eligibility.

The announcements created an uproar, but the impact was positive and immediate. Within a few days, the vaccination reports from around the country were arriving much quicker and looked much more comprehensive. Each day, the numbers of the vaccinated were increasing by an interval greater than the previous day. The numbers had jumped from 300–400 thousand vaccinations per day to the point that we were approaching a million. Internally, we were hoping to hit a million reported vaccinations a day prior to our departure on January 20. On January 20, the reported number of vaccinations exceeded 1.5 million.[15]

The changes we decided on in early January had their intended effect. After January 12, governors, mayors, and public health officials began reaching out to us in large numbers, claiming their vaccination numbers "were wrong," that we had underreported how well they were doing. Of course, the only source of vaccination numbers was the jurisdictions themselves, and we were easily able to verify every report we had received from every one of them. There were likely tough conversations taking place all over the country. The governors, mayors, and other leaders were now highly engaged. They were making changes of their own, for the better.

10

LESSONS UPON LEAVING

VARIANTS

COVID variants began appearing in mid-2021 and, with them, a spike in cases and deaths. Alarm followed, but so, too, did a sense of urgency among the unvaccinated to get their shots.

According to a state-by-state study released from the highly respected and independent Kaiser Family Foundation at the end of July, "The rates of death among fully vaccinated persons with COVID-19 [are] effectively zero (0.00%) in all but two reporting states, Arkansas and Michigan where they were 0.01%" and, the Foundation added, those "[d]eaths may or may not have been due to COVID-19."[1]

In short, the vaccines continued to work and work well, against the variants, too. Those who are unvaccinated, particularly the older and more vulnerable for other reasons of health, should talk to their doctor about getting theirs.

FAREWELL TO THE TEAM

After nearly eight months together, engaged in a valiant struggle against a deadly virus, January 20 was rapidly approaching, and the team that had bonded so deeply, and achieved so much together *as a team,* was breaking up. The Biden administration had decided to keep the Army Material Command component under General Perna intact. Carlo de Notaristefani, our senior manufacturing expert, would stay as well. Every political appointee—Secretary Azar, Bob Kadlec, Dr. Redfield and me—was to hand in his badge at noon on January 20. A couple of weeks earlier, the Biden folks had decided they would dismiss Moncef Slaoui and replace him with David Kessler, who had been the FDA commissioner years before but knew nothing of vaccines.[2]

On the same day as the January 12 press conference, Dr. Slaoui bade us all farewell. We were on the seventh floor of the Humphrey Building in an area specially designated for the core Operation Warp Speed team. General Perna, after having served close to forty years in the military, understood deeply the importance of these events. Every unit in the Army conducted similar events known as "Hail and Farewells" as a means of formally welcoming new officers into the unit and thanking those who were finishing their tours.

As fifteen or twenty officers gathered around, General Perna formally thanked Moncef for all he had done and especially for his partnership. We would not have been anywhere close to where we were in terms of achievement if these two gentlemen, each from very different worlds and backgrounds, had not collaborated so famously and so seamlessly. General Perna offered Moncef a number of mementos, and then it was time for Moncef to address the group.

Recall that Moncef Slaoui was born in Morocco and largely educated in Europe. He only came to the United States as an adult. Yet he had been thrust into the most important role of his lifetime as part of a team that would save hundreds of thousands of American lives and set new records for vaccine development, manufacturing, and distribution.

It was an emotional moment for Moncef and for all of us. He did not wish to leave his team, and no one there wanted him to go. When he began to speak, he was understandably a bit choked up. Beyond what we would have expected, he talked about his deep, newfound appreciation for the United States Army, its sense of mission, commitment, and camaraderie. His words were heartfelt and sincere, which was not surprising to anyone who knew him. There was nothing but mutual respect in that room at that moment.

As I heard him speak, I remembered my own days as a young Army artillery officer and thought, "Damn, Moncef took the words right out of my mouth." Reconnecting with the United States Army for me was a fabulous aspect of an otherwise very tragic year. General Perna was about the same year group as I was, so we had a number of mutual acquaintances, including the Army Chief of Staff, General Jim McConville, who was my classmate at West Point. But it was also the more junior officers who were so inspiring. These included Tony McQueen, Ted Shinkle, Jesse Marsalis, Matt Alexander, Deacon Maddox, Doug Meyer, and RJ Mikesh. These officers, ranging from major to full colonel, had grown up in an Army constantly at war. For their entire careers, they had been engaged in post 9/11 conflict in the Middle East. This was a resilient bunch, whose members dug right in and never let up.

The final days before January 20 were disrupted by the Secret Service and its preparations for the upcoming inauguration of a new president. Being adjacent to the United States Capitol, the Humphrey Building fell within the security bubble. As of Friday, January 16, there would be no cars entering or leaving the garage beneath the building. Our offices needed to be cleared of all files, and entry in the building would be for essential activity only. For the first time in eight months, many of the Operation Warp Speed team members worked from home.

There are only a couple of opportunities in most of our lives to experience a true *team performance*. The characteristics of such performances are simple but often elusive: a clear and compelling mission, a sense of mutual accountability to each other, an intense level of commitment, complementary skills among those on the team, and every participant subordinating his own interests to that of the mission. These characteristics create lifelong bonds among a team's members. How could one not feel privileged and honored to have been part of such a team? Those were my feelings at noon on January 20, 2021.

POLITICIZING AN EXCEPTIONAL AMERICAN ACHIEVEMENT

The Biden folks entered office, claiming to want to heal, rather than further divide the American people, but, from my perspective, that spirit ended at about 1:00 p.m. on January 20. They were quick to disparage all Operation Warp Speed had accomplished for the political purpose of elevating their own role in vaccinating the nation. They even scrapped the name "Operation Warp Speed,"[3] although it will remain the popular moniker of the most successful vaccine development, manufacturing, distribution, and administration effort in history. The media, to its credit, continues to use the term to this day.

Of course, several of the quotations coming from the new occupants of the White House were from "anonymous figures," who apparently did not have enough courage of their convictions to attach their names. As it related to Operation Warp Speed, the American people were told that the Biden folks were "left a mess,"[4] that we "had left them no plan to vaccinate Americans," and, the biggest whopper of them all, "[the Biden administration] had to start from scratch."[5]

Recall that we had already secured hundreds of millions of safe and effective vaccine doses ready for use, set up or expanded twenty-seven manufacturing facilities, ushered the vaccine candidates through very large and successful clinical trials, procured all of the needles, syringes, vials, and dry ice necessary to store, distribute, and vaccinate all Americans, helped to craft the sixty-four public-health jurisdiction vaccination plans, and had designed the most sophisticated vaccine tracking system ever used in the United States. And we had done all of this in record time. As of January 20, the CDC reported that over 1.5 million Americans were vaccinated in the prior 24 hours. Meanwhile, more than a million doses of vaccine were being shipped from our factories each day. The Biden folks' derogatory comments were all the more perplexing and ironic given the context of the Biden team's prior experience in dealing with pandemic responses and, as mentioned previously, that none of them showed up in person to execute a smooth transition. In April 2009, the Obama-Biden administration faced the H1N1 virus—a cousin of the Spanish Flu that was thought ready to run riot throughout the world. In the end the virus turned out to be far less lethal than feared, but as their man-in-charge of the response, current White House chief of staff Ron Klain told a Texas A&M symposium in 2019:

> We did every possible thing wrong. Sixty million Americans got H1N1 in that period of time, and it is just purely a fortuity that this isn't one of the great mass-casualty events in American history. [It] had nothing to do with us doing anything right; just had to do with luck. If anyone thinks that can't happen again, they don't have to go back to [the Spanish Flu of] 1918. Just go back to 2009, 2010. Imagine a virus with a different lethality, and you can just do the math.[6]

The Biden people subsequently pledged they would achieve "100 million vaccinations in 100 days."[7] Well, they would have had to have diminished the pace we had left them to get to only 100 million. An appropriate football metaphor would be that the Trump administration drove the ball ninety-nine yards down the field to the one-yard line. Then, a new quarterback entered the game with a first and goal on the one-yard line. Yes, they leaned forward and fell into the end-zone, but that was it.

At some point, the Biden administration comments were so absurd they were reminiscent of "Baghdad Bob" in 2003. As American M1

Abrams tanks were rolling down the main boulevards of Baghdad uncontested, "Bob" was telling the Iraqi people not to worry; our Imperial Guard is successfully driving back the Americans.[8]

The Biden administration deserves credit for finishing the job. There is no doubt about that. They could have fumbled the ball on the one-yard line. But to constantly disparage the work we did was a shameless politicization of a uniquely unifying national achievement. It also did nothing to enhance vaccine confidence, an issue that has confounded the new administration. Moreover, it demonstrated a lack of executive presence on the part of the newly inaugurated president.

Had his career ever included any executive leadership roles, he probably would have realized the impact the criticisms his team was levelling had on the morale of the hundreds of military officers and career officials who had given their all for the previous eight months on behalf of the American people. These professionals were still there, working day, night, and weekends to deliver vaccines, yet they were under a barrage of criticism from their own commander-in-chief's team. And for what? Short-term political gain. President Biden appears to be a good man, but he was clearly getting poor advice on this matter.

Months into the Biden administration's tenure, when I would speak with my former teammates who were still on the job, they consistently claimed that very little, if anything, had changed from the vaccine distribution and administration plan we had left them. The September 2020 CDC vaccine distribution operating playbook clearly described three phases, each broadening the access points and eligibility criteria over time.[9] The Biden folks have followed this plan religiously, expanding the use of retail pharmacies and other distribution points, while loosening eligibility criteria.

There were two exceptions though. The Biden team introduced Federal Emergency Management Agency–operated mass vaccination sites. Biden pledged 100 of these. They never fully materialized and eventually shut down.[10] Second, they initiated a door-to-door knocking campaign to try to increase awareness of vaccine access. As one can imagine, this did not go over well. I would not criticize them, though. Any reasonable attempt to get more Americans vaccinated quickly was worth a try. Similar to us in trial-and-error, the Biden folks adapted when they learned the mass vaccination sites and door-to-door campaign were belly flops.

So, in the end, the Biden folks *publicly* disparaged and dismissed our plans but *privately* embraced nearly every aspect of what was developed under President Trump. As I have grown accustomed to saying, "They snubbed their noses at the Trump dog food at night, but the bowl was always empty in the morning."

PROMISES MADE, PROMISE KEPT

Throughout the fall 2020, the one question the media posed to us more than any other was, "When will all Americans be able to get vaccinated?" From President Trump, to General Perna, to Dr. Slaoui, to Secretary Azar, and even down to my bi-weekly Hill and press briefings, we consistently pegged the date as the end of the second quarter (June 30) 2021.[11]

We believed that the combination of ramped-up manufacturing and producing up to four vaccines with emergency use authorizations would be sufficient to accomplish this objective. We were particularly excited about the impending approval of the J&J vaccine. It was a single-dose vaccine, and its technology platform made manufacturing it highly scalable. It was also the easiest to store and transport.

Of course, there would be disruptions, as there were temporarily with J&J and the persistent problems at AstraZeneca. But this brings us back to the initial strategy Dr. Slaoui developed in the summer 2020—backing six vaccine candidates divided into three different technology platforms. We were criticized for not doubling down more, and earlier, on producing additional Pfizer and Moderna vaccine doses. Those criticisms had the benefit of twenty-twenty hindsight.

In July and August of 2020, we had no idea how well or poorly any single vaccine would perform in clinical trials, whether it would be effective in those over age sixty-five, or whether it could be manufactured effectively at large scale. What we did know was that we had a very high probability (75%) of achieving at least one safe and effective vaccine, manufactured at scale, and effective in those over age sixty-five by year's end. Once we saw which vaccines would be winners, we would be able to concentrate raw material and production capacity on those.

In the end, we achieved our objective: any American desiring a vaccine had access to one before June 30, 2021.[12] At a time when virtually every other western developed country, and of course, those which were less developed, was still struggling to get enough vaccines to its people, the American economy was opening. Life was returning to normal.

The Biden administration pledged to allow folks to have a backyard barbeque by Independence Day 2021.[13] They pegged the date a little late. Americans started firing up their grills around Memorial Day.

The Trump administration made a commitment to the American people. We delivered on it.

This leads me back to the Rose Garden event on May 15, 2020, the official kickoff of Operation Warp Speed. Moncef Slaoui had to make a critical decision. With the whole world watching, he decided without much forethought that he would "jump off the cliff," as he described it, and commit unconditionally to delivering vaccines before the end of 2020. He was officially departing from his lifetime role as a scientific genius and the world's most successful vaccine developer. He chose instead to be a leader, and the leadership he demonstrated on that humid day in May is uncommon in Washington. He chose to set the bar of expectations impossibly high, even at the risk of ridicule and failing to meet them. Most in Washington do the opposite. They set very low expectations, hoping to exceed them.

IF WE COULD TURN BACK TIME

In the spring and summer of 2021, I spent a lot of time interviewing my former Operation Warp Speed colleagues about their thoughts and reflections on the effort. Most commented that it was the single best team experience of their lives. That was true for me, too.

However, I had to pose an uncomfortable question as well. "What would you have done differently if we could start over again?" There were several answers that, on the margin, would have made some difference. We could have organized the Operation Warp Speed effort a little earlier. We should have pressed our case with the manufacturers contracting with Emergent when we uncovered the potential for breakdown. We could have entered phase III clinical trials with Moderna a week or two earlier.

By far, however, the most consistent response dealt with vaccine hesitancy. Should we have communicated more aggressively and earlier? Should we have had a "communications lead" at the level of a General Perna or a Dr. Slaoui? (We eventually had Michael Pratt from HHS's public affairs unit. Michael very capably filled this role, but perhaps we brought him too late into the game.)

In the late summer 2020, we allocated $300 million to a campaign designed to enhance vaccine acceptance, yet we wound up not using much of it before December, when the first vaccines were granted emergency use authorizations.

We were also experiencing turmoil and turnover, to say the least, in the HHS public affairs function. We conducted several meetings during the summer of 2020 on this topic and debated different points of view. We concluded that there would be risk in spending months building excitement about the imminent arrival of safe and effective vaccines only to have the vaccine candidates fail.

We were also concerned that, even if successful, upon emergency use authorization approval, we would not have enough doses immediately to meet all the demand. In December, and then throughout the winter of 2021, this was certainly true. We had tracked manufacturing numbers throughout the fall and anticipated having 40 million doses available by the end of the year. For starters, there were 55–60 million vulnerable seniors in the country, so we would not have been able to satisfy even them.

Given this, we did begin a set of "narrowcast," rather than broadcast, activities through a vaccine advisory council. Laura Trueman had the lead. This council had superb representation from minority communities, including such organizations as the historically Black colleges and universities (HBCU). We anticipated hesitancy in this demographic.[14] Yet while this narrowcast effort was without question helpful, it was clearly insufficient.

The issue of vaccine hesitancy persisted well into the Biden administration's tenure. Prone to setting low expectations so they could exceed them, the Biden team established a target of 70 percent of eligible Americans vaccinated by July 4, 2021, weekend, yet came up significantly short.[15]

My personal observations suggest three major shortcomings with the federal government's capability in influencing the behavior of its citizens. The most obvious of these is lack of trust. I will not itemize all the legitimate reasons for this over decades, but it is real. By their comments throughout the 2020 campaign season, President Biden, Vice President Harris, and Governor Cuomo were sure to have further eroded trust in these government-sponsored vaccines.

Second, while we had great medical scientists and practitioners working both within the Operation Warp Speed team and the larger pandemic response team, to my knowledge we did not have a single behavioral scientist. Behavioral science has become a serious discipline with proven principles. Repeatedly going on television to preach at Americans to wear a mask or get vaccinated, whether one is the president of the United States or the world's leading virologist, simply does not work. There are many behavioral science principles such as "status quo bias," "salience bias," and "loss aversion" that were not employed systematically during the COVID response. They should have been.

Perhaps most significant though, the federal government is at least one decade behind the American people and big technology companies when it comes to the strategic use of social media. The government's social media presence is severely lacking. At HHS, before the pandemic, we were hard-pressed to find within our agencies a level of social media followers exceeding hundreds of thousands. Medicare alone has close to 60 million beneficiaries, yet the CMS Facebook page, the social medium most used by seniors, in 2019 had fewer than 500,000 followers.

So while the country has grown accustomed to mobile applications, real-time exchange of information on social media platforms, and how to identify what was trending among the American people, the federal government was still relying on traditional media, web pages, and "authoritative voices," such as Drs. Fauci and Birx.

This deficiency in social media presence, social media listening, and social media influencing could have deleterious impact well beyond pandemic response and vaccinations. I hope Congress will take note.

LESSONS LEARNED FOR THE NEXT PANDEMIC

For all the reasons I have chosen to write about the experiences of Operation Warp Speed, perhaps the most important is the lessons we learned that will (hopefully) permit us to cope more effectively with the next pandemic. Serious attention to lessons learned may be a harbinger for good government processes and governance in general. I see particularly important lessons as they relate to establishing well-functioning public-private partnerships.

Lesson one: Assemble the Right Talent and Create a Genuine Team

As I wrote at the opening, Operation Warp Speed was not principally the result of good fortune or random occurrence as much as it was the product of outstanding leadership, a coherent strategy, exacting execution, exceptional teamwork, and a unique public-private partnership. It started with a multidisciplinary team of professional leaders comprising complementary skills, and support for this started at the top.

If one can get past all the media hype and constant criticism about President Trump, what one finds is an experienced business leader and dealmaker, the first real career businessman-as-president in our history. He had a fundamental belief in the private sector, its ability to innovate, and its ability to mobilize. He knew this because he had experienced it.

This was clear early in the pandemic. We thought we would be short of mechanical ventilators for patients in intensive care units. In a matter of 90–120 days, as a result of the president's public and behind-the-scenes efforts, Ford, General Motors, and others, spit out over 100,000 new ventilators, in many cases converting their factories to do it. The installed base of ventilators in US hospitals just before the crisis was estimated to be approximately 80,000. Trump was also a delegator. He gave his team general guidance, provided the support it needed, but did not micromanage.

Next in line was Alex Azar, a Health and Human Services secretary with over a decade of senior leadership experience in the pharmaceutical industry and experience in dealing with pandemic threats in a previous stint at HHS under President George W. Bush. Prior secretaries generally came from the ranks of governors or congressmen, or otherwise in the public service domain. No prior secretary in the history of the Department had such industry experience as Azar did. Critically, he understood the economics, risk tolerance, and decision-making processes that guided one of America's largest industrial sectors, pharmaceuticals. He also understood that we did not have the talent necessary within the government to achieve our aspirations.

Next was General Gus Perna and his team of logisticians led by Paul Ostrowski and Chris Sharpsten. As mentioned, they had been supporting combat operations in the Middle East almost continuously for two decades. These talented officers understood that overlooking the smallest detail could result in lost lives. They were all about exacting planning, rehearsal, and execution.

Then, of course, there were Moncef Slaoui, Matt Hepburn, and Carlo de Notaristefani, all recognized experts in the fields of vaccine development and manufacturing, respectively. This was the talent Secretary Azar knew we needed but did not possess within the Department of Health and Human Services.

Of course, there was Bob Kadlec. We used to refer to him as "Ready, Fire, Aim," but his impulses were almost always spot on. He was heavily criticized early in the pandemic for ordering approximately 600 million cotton face masks from the underwear maker Hanes.[16] We jokingly referred to them as "face panties." However, when we wanted kids going back to school in the fall of 2020, shipping tens of millions of these face masks out to the states and down to the school districts did a lot to mitigate the risk. Bob was the one who secured needles, syringes, and vials for vaccines before anyone else was thinking about them.

Then there was a bevy of other instrumental team players. Jared Kushner and his talented young sidekicks, Adam Boehler and Brad Smith always had our backs at the White House. Greg D'Angelo at OMB and his boss Russ Vought, along with Jen Moughalian at HHS, worked their magic to get us the funding for Operation Warp Speed, despite Speaker Pelosi's slow walking of the supplemental package in the fall of 2020. Secretary Mark Esper, and then Deputy Secretary David Norquist, committed an immense amount of Defense Department resources without question to the effort. And, despite the contentious relationship with Dr. Messonnier at the CDC, several of her direct reports, such as Anita Patel and Amanda Cohen, were exceptional team players.

Aggregating exceptional talent alone does not necessarily create a team. Indeed, the opposite often occurs. One need look no further than many professional sports teams all possessing exceptional talent, but only a few of which win consistently. The difference is almost always the sense of team demonstrated by the winners. What are some of these characteristics?

It starts with the absence of egos. As mentioned earlier, there could not have been two more humble leaders in Washington, DC, in 2020 than Gus Perna and Moncef Slaoui. As Moncef commented during his interview with us in April of 2020, "I take responsibility for all of our failures and give credit to others for our successes." Gus Perna personified this every day as well. Second, trust and delegation: President Trump trusted Secretary Azar to get the job done, and Secretary Azar trusted the day-to-day working team to get the job done. But the OWS team went beyond these characteristics. There was a genuine sense of respect and mutual admiration for what each brought to the table. Most of its members were seasoned professionals, battle-tested in their own respective environments over decades. They had nothing more to prove to themselves. Fulfillment came from saving the country.

So, we had the combination of relevant private sector experience, vaccine development and manufacturing expertise, career government expertise, the best logistics team in the world, and just enough take-that-hill attitude to be successful. Lesson number one, therefore, is "assemble the right talent and forge them into a team."

Lesson Two: Articulate a Clear, Compelling Vision

If anyone, at any time, asked a member of the Operation Warp Speed team what he was trying to accomplish, one would have heard precisely the same answer: "Deliver at least one safe and effective vaccine, manufactured at scale, and distributed to sixty-four jurisdictions before year's end 2020." Everyone on the team knew precisely what was at stake: saving American lives.

Of course, the chief tasks were broken down into the three major areas of vaccine development, vaccine manufacturing, and vaccine distribution, but everyone was intently focused on the singular goal. This vision focused all our activities and decisions, ranging from the vaccine candidates Dr. Slaoui selected, to the partners Generals Perna and Ostrowski selected, to the planning conducted by the CDC, to the funding requirements, to the pace at which Tiberius needed to be developed, and to all our internal processes and performance management systems. When there is no ambiguity about what the goal is, the members of the team can essentially manage themselves, and this is what we experienced.

The Operation Warp Speed leaders had an immense coordination challenge, but because of a well-understood, compelling vision, it was a much less demanding people-management challenge.

Lesson Three: Obey the Laws of Comparative Advantage

The "law of comparative advantage" is a complex economic concept, but I will hijack the term and apply it to what became one of the most successful public-private partnerships in history. The federal government's role in Operation Warp Speed reflected a philosophical belief that it should do only what the private sector *cannot do* better. We were exquisitely sensitive to the concept of never letting our reach exceed our grasp. There were no authoritarian impulses on the team, and, indeed, as I mentioned, there was an inveterate belief in the power of the private sector. Therefore, with few exceptions, such as the Veterans' Administration and the Department of Defense, no federal employee was directly involved in manufacturing, packaging, shipping, or injecting a single dose of any Warp Speed COVID vaccine. The doses generally went from factory to McKesson, to UPS or FedEx, directly to the point of vaccination, which was often a retail pharmacy. With few exceptions, we never took physical possession of the vaccines.

Our role was clear: enable the private sector to be successful. We did this by assuming financial risks private industry would not tolerate. We also chose to utilize tried and tested systems and processes that had been honed for decades by private industry whenever possible. Specifically, we let one of the biggest pharmaceutical distributors in the world (McKesson) handle the vaccines, let the most successful delivery companies in the world (UPS and FedEx) deliver the vaccines, let those entities who knew best how to vaccinate millions of Americans (CVS and Walgreens) conduct vaccinations.

Where we had assets in place, such as NIH-approved clinical trial sites, we put them in play. When we needed to accelerate the delivery of critical equipment from all over the world, we used military-chartered air to go and get it. When we needed to reprioritize the use of raw materials, equipment, and labor, we used the Defense Production Act.

The law of comparative advantage also extended to our relationships with the sixty-four public-health jurisdictions. Again, we were criticized for not developing a one-size-fits-all federal government plan to administer close to 600 million vaccine doses, but we firmly believed that governors, mayors, county commissioners, and township supervisors knew their geographies, their priorities, and their populations better than the federal government ever could. The states will always be our laboratories of innovation if we permit them to play this role. Sure, it took them three or four weeks to understand whether their assumptions about vaccine uptake, access, and prioritization played out as intended, but when reality did not align with plans in many cases, these state and local leaders adapted quickly. In less than 180 days' time, the jurisdictions administered over 300 million vaccine doses.[17]

Lesson Four: Govern to Bypass the Bureaucracy

Bureaucracies serve a valuable purpose in a complex environment. They divide tasks and roles into minute clusters, permitting career officials in this case to develop the extraordinarily deep levels of knowledge necessary to deal with the complexity. However, this often creates organizational silos, and integrating all these silos to deliver a well-vetted, comprehensive outcome takes time. We did not have the luxury of time, so we had to suspend the normal bureaucratic processes. We traded speed for the risk of perhaps missing some aspect of relevant input from either somewhere in the Executive Office Building or another cabinet-level department. Given what was at stake, we thought it was an appropriate trade-off, and we mitigated the risks by actively keeping others informed but not inviting them into the decision-making process.

A classic example of this was with the National Security Council. My counterpart there, Brian Cavanaugh, set up weekly sessions with his entire NSC team, and I would provide a detailed update on progress. At the same time, I would obtain their input. I did the same thing with OMB and with Brad Smith, who was representing the Domestic Policy Council. We even occasionally updated the Council of Economic Advisors.

The two central aspects of our governance structure, however, were first the Operation Warp Speed board, comprising elements from Health and Human Services, Department of Defense, and the White House, and second, we had a direct line to the Oval Office through Jared.

The Operation Warp Speed board essentially met once per week, on Friday mornings, to review both vaccine and therapeutic developments. All week-to-week tactical decisions were adjudicated there. For major decisions and updates, a small group of us went over to the Oval Office (approximately once a month). Given the Rose Garden event in May, there was little doubt across the entire government regarding how much the president was behind the effort. His door was always open to us. All we needed to do was call Jared.

Lesson Five: If You Design a "Skunk Works," Let the Skunks Do Their Thing

For several decades, American businesses have employed the concept of a "skunk works" to accelerate the pace at which innovation occurs. A skunk works typically involves assembling a multidisciplinary team whose members do not normally work with each other, sequestering them in a common facility, providing the resources they need to be successful, and protecting them from distractions. Sound familiar?

Shortly after the May kickoff in the Rose Garden, the requests started streaming in from the media, from the Hill, from the private sector, and from elements at the White House, such as the White House Task Force. Everyone wanted some of Secretary Azar's, General Perna's or Dr. Slaoui's time. To fulfill all these requests would have meant spending little or even no time on what we most needed to do: deliver tens of millions of safe and effective vaccines to the American people before year's end 2020. So we created proxies. Bob Redfield and I would update the White House Task Force. Paul Ostrowski and I would brief the media and the Hill every other Thursday. And Bob Kadlec and a few others would handle many of the private-sector requests. Paul Ostrowski also handled media interactions for General Perna.

General Perna and Dr. Slaoui set up two key multi-hour meetings per week. One reviewed detailed progress on therapeutics and the other on vaccines. He invited proxies, such as Dr. Kadlec, a representative named Grace Bruno from OMB, and me to attend. This gave all of us the information we needed for that week to represent them in front of other stakeholders.

These five lessons may not sound revolutionary to many of the highest-performing corporations in the world, but they represent a radical departure from the way the federal government typically does business. Again, it started at the top with the first true businessman-turned-president in US history. And it continued down the line with the likes of Alex Azar, Jared Kushner, Adam Boehler, Brad Smith, Moncef Slaoui, and Carlo de Notaristefani, all seasoned business entrepreneurs or executives. The mindset, structure, and processes we created were those found in the private sector.

I hope the federal government draws from these lessons for other consequential undertakings in the future.

PERSONAL REFLECTIONS

On May 27, 1981, under a clear blue sky at Michie Stadium, President Ronald Reagan handed me my diploma as I graduated from West Point. When one considers the series of government-led failures and disappointments during the years leading up to that event, to include Watergate, a humiliating withdrawal from Vietnam, runaway inflation with an economy in shambles, a narrative describing the United States as being in a state of "malaise," and then the failed rescue attempt of our hostages in Iran, President Reagan's presence could have been nothing but inspiring and invigorating. He said in his 1980 GOP convention acceptance speech that he was going to make America great again, and he did. Indeed, rather than claiming the government would save America, he was clear that only Americans could save America. He often referred to the government as the *source* of our problems, not the solution. He was a limited-government president. Scarcely four months into his presidency and two months following the assassination attempt on his life, we, as a country, were optimistic again. He delivered a long address that day, but I distilled it down to two messages: thank you for serving your country, and I'm going to make you proud of it again. His optimism about America made a deep impression on me, one that has persisted for over forty years.

There was another man on the dais that day, the superintendent of the United States Military Academy, Lieutenant General Andrew Goodpaster. With the Academy in turmoil in the mid-seventies from both a major cheating scandal and the then-controversial admission of the first women, LTG Goodpaster gave up his fourth star, exited retirement, and returned to the Academy as its fifty-first superintendent in 1977, the same year I arrived as a plebe.

Goodpastor made it clear to us early in our cadet years that no matter what we did after graduation, whether serving in the military or returning to civilian life, the obligation we incurred by attending West Point was "a life of service and dedication to the country." This ethic of service to the nation he had demonstrated for decades also made a deep impression on me.

These two men, coming from vastly different backgrounds, shared a common task. They both needed to lead turnarounds of major institutions in which the public had lost faith. They were both cognizant of, and motivated by, a keen sense of mission. They both subscribed to a simple set of principles. They were both great communicators.

Given these experiences in my foundational years, it was an easy decision when Alex Azar, the newly confirmed secretary of Health and Human Services, called me in the late spring of 2018 and asked if I wanted to serve the federal government as part of his staff. Of course, neither of us had any idea what the depths of that service would be until we received that fateful phone call from Bob Redfield on January 3, 2020, informing us that he thought there was a "problem in China."

When former colleagues and others ask me about being part of the pandemic response and Operation Warp Speed, I start by telling them it was a distinct privilege, and I mean it. What an honor it was to serve with such a talented, committed group of professionals on such a meaningful mission. I then go on to tell them that the United States government is a study in contrasts. It has serious limitations when it comes to understanding the motivations of its people and the diversity of experiences that cause them to, for instance, wear a mask or choose not to. In Washington, DC, there is a level of elitist, "inside the beltway" thinking contributing to these limitations. On the other hand, I tell them, when its use is targeted and limited, the federal government can be immensely powerful, particularly when "its reach does not exceed its grasp." When it assembles the talent, knowledge, and sense of commitment inherent in its people, gives them the necessary resources, and trusts them to get the job done, it can achieve the seemingly impossible.

I wrote this book focusing on the latter, the immense convening power and targeted use of federal government resources as a force and catalyst for good. What other organization could muster the diverse talent from both the public and private sector at the same place at the same time, in support of such an important mission? And what a melting pot of talent that was: a chief scientific advisor from Morocco, a manufacturing expert from Italy, a secretary of Arab-Lebanese heritage, an assistant secretary whose Czech parents met in a forced labor camp during World War II, and a street-fighting, four-star general from New Jersey. What were the odds all these leaders would forge unbreakable bonds in support of a common goal? What were the odds they would, to a person, subordinate their egos to save the nation from further catastrophe? What other organization could mobilize private industry quickly and effectively to deliver the American people from such a catastrophic pandemic?

From supporting the design of vaccine vials containing glass capable of handling –80-degree Celsius temperatures without shattering, to setting up or expanding twenty-seven manufacturing facilities in less than seven months, to developing temperature and motion-sensitive, GPS-tracked delivery containers for precious vaccines, to achieving over 99.99 percent on-time delivery of those containers to the right place under the correct storage conditions: where else in the world could innovation have occurred so quickly and effectively?

And, of course, what other organization could easily justify a near-infinite return on a $30 billion-plus investment? With the largest economy in the world operating at half-speed in March and April of

2020, the US Treasury was losing $6–7 billion *a day* in tax revenue. If getting the American people vaccinated would permit the US economy to fully reopen, the cost of Operation Warp Speed, at approximately $30 billion, returned that investment in approximately a week's time.

As evidenced by the fact that we were the only country in the world that developed, produced, and distributed enough doses of vaccine to ensure every citizen who wanted one could get it before the end of the second quarter of 2021, it became clear that no other country possessed the combination of exceptional leadership, pace of innovation, industrial dexterity, and human capital that we found here in the United States. This is what I hope the reader takes away: when used appropriately and for good, when led by selfless servants and when transformed to bypass the normal bureaucratic processes, the federal government and the American people can achieve the seemingly impossible. Winning world wars, landing on the moon, delivering hundreds of millions of doses of safe and effective vaccine scarcely a year after the identification of a deadly virus? No problem.

My involvement in Operation Warp Speed was simple. It was the partial fulfillment of an obligation I incurred over forty years before when I raised my right hand on The Plain at West Point for the first time. For the reader, I hope this account will lead to some well-needed optimism, the same level of optimism President Reagan instilled in me so many years ago. Among all the political strife, criticism of our country's imperfections, and intolerance for diverse perspectives, constantly carried across multiple traditional and social media channels, I hope you will find the commitment, sacrifice, and accomplishments of those involved with Operation Warp Speed, with tremendous, yet targeted, support from their government, both inspiring and a source of pride again in being an American.

ACKNOWLEDGMENTS

My wife Dawn and daughter Eve endured a good part of the pandemic alone in Pittsburgh while I was in Washington, DC. At one point, I went several months without seeing either of them; for my wife and me, this was the longest stretch of not seeing each other in our almost forty years of marriage. I thank them for their resilience during a very difficult period.

Grace-Marie Turner of The Galen Institute is not someone who takes no for an answer, and that is why, in large part, she is responsible for this book having been written. When several publishers refused to even consider evaluating an Operation Warp Speed manuscript from a former Trump official, she called Alex Hoyt, who eventually became my agent, who called Al Regnery, whose company, Republic Book Publishers, enthusiastically embraced the concept. A very special thanks to Grace-Marie for her persistence and for her long-standing friendship. I offer special thanks as well to Al Regnery, Eric Kampmann, and their colleagues at Republic for their support, advice, and professionalism. As a first-time author, I very much appreciated their counsel.

Clark Judge and his colleague, Lucy Van Schaijik, at the White House Writers Group have been fabulous partners from the start. Clark took my stream of consciousness and molded it into a coherent narrative. Lucy tracked down and verified over two hundred citations, among other tasks. They invested much more time in this publication than that for which they were compensated, which is a testament to the values they share.

Many of my Operation Warp Speed teammates spent hours with me throughout the spring and summer of 2021 being interviewed about their own backgrounds, experiences, what led them to become part of the Operation Warp Speed team, and how they felt at certain points throughout the effort. These include Alex Azar, Bob Kadlec, Moncef Slaoui, Matt Hepburn, Garrett Grigsby, Peter Marks, Francis Collins, Greg D'Angelo, Carlo de Notaristefani, and several others whose names I pledged to keep confidential. I also received input from Mark Esper. Many, many thanks to each of you. Your backgrounds are fascinating, and your perspectives were invaluable to capturing many details I would have missed.

Thanks as well to Senator Tom Cotton for composing the foreword to this book. He and his policy lead, Brian Colas, were very gracious during my time at Health and Human Services, always offering keen insights and perspectives on key issues.

Lastly, thanks to my former colleagues Brian Harrison, Judy Stecker, and Catherine Bird from the HHS Chief of Staff's Office. While I was off handling Operation Warp Speed issues for most of 2020, they were picking up the slack for me as it related to my other duties as the Deputy Chief of Staff for Policy. It was a 100 percent team effort.

ENDNOTES

INTRODUCTION

1 "1918 Pandemic (H1N1 Virus)." Centers for Disease Control and Prevention. Centers for Disease Control and Prevention, March 20, 2019. https://www.cdc.gov/flu/pandemic-resources/1918-pandemic-h1n1.html.

2 "U.S. Covid-19 'Vaccine Diplomacy' Is Catching up to China and Russia's Efforts." MSNBC. NBCUniversal News Group, July 7, 2021. https://www.msnbc.com/opinion/u-s-covid-19-vaccine-diplomacy-catching-china-russia-s-n1272957.

3 "Vaccinations Against COVID-19 May Have Averted Up To 140,000 Deaths In The United States", Health Affairs, August 18, 2021. Authors: Gupta, Cantor, Simon, Bento, Wing, and Whaley".

4 Katella, Kathy. "Comparing the COVID-19 Vaccines: How Are They Different?" Yale Medicine. Yale Medicine, November 3, 2021. https://www.yalemedicine.org/news/covid-19-vaccine-comparison.

5 "Press Briefing by White House COVID-19 Response Team and Public Health Officials." The White House. The United States Government, November 10, 2021. https://www.whitehouse.gov/briefing-room/press-briefings/2021/11/10/press-briefing-by-white-house-covid-19-response-team-and-public-health-officials-67/.

6 Mulligan, Casey B., and Tomas J. Philipson. "Opinion | Government Failure Gave the World Covid." The Wall Street Journal. Dow Jones & Company, August 9, 2021. https://www.wsj.com/articles/fauci-wuhan-institute-virology-covid-origins-negative-externalities-lockdowns-masks-11628524500.

7 Scott, Dylan. "Trump's Operation Warp Speed Could Be a Success. the Problem Is Trump." *Vox,* Vox, 7 Oct. 2020, www.vox.com/coronavirus-covid19/2020/10/7/21504134/trump-covid-19-vaccine-operation-warp-speed-debate.

8 "Meet the First Person in the US to Get COVID Vaccine." Kaiser Health News, December 15, 2020. https://khn.org/morning-breakout/meet-the-first-person-in-the-us-to-get-covid-vaccine/.

9 Spalding, Rebecca, and Carl O'Donnell. "U.S. Vaccinations in 2020 Fall Far Short of Target of 20 Million People." Reuters. Thomson Reuters, December 31, 2020. https://www.reuters.com/article/us-health-coronavirus-usa-vaccinations/u-svaccinations-in-2020-fall-far-short-of-target-of-20-million-people-idUSKBN29512W.

10 Thompson, Stuart A. "How Long Will a Vaccine Really Take?" *The New York Times,* The New York Times, 30 Apr. 2020, www.nytimes.com/interactive/2020/04/30/opinion/coronavirus-covid-vaccine.html.

11 "'Vaccine or No Vaccine." TRANSCRIPT: 5/15/20, The 11th Hour with Brian Williams." MSNBC, NBCUniversal News Group, 17 Sept. 2020, www.msnbc.com/transcripts/11th-hour-with-brian-williams/2020–05–15-msna1357836.

12 Emanuel, Ezekiel J., and Paul A. Offit. "Could Trump Turn a Vaccine into a Campaign Stunt?" The New York Times. The New York Times, June 8, 2020. https://www.nytimes.com/2020/06/08/opinion/trump-coronavirus-vaccine.html.

13 "Joe Biden Says He Doesn't Trust President Trump on Coronavirus Vaccine Development, Calls for Transparency." *C,* www.c-span.org/video/?475890–1%2Fjoe-biden-trust-president-trump-coronavirus-vaccine-development-calls-transparency.

14 Jarvis, Jacob. "Kamala Harris Doesn't Trust Trump's Word on Vaccines. She's Not Alone." *Newsweek,* Newsweek, 8 Oct. 2020, www.newsweek.com/kamala-harris-doesnt-trust-trump-vaccines-1537331.

15 Sullivan, Kate. "Biden Receives First Dose of Covid-19 Vaccine on Live Television." *CNN,* Cable News Network, 21 Dec. 2020, www.cnn.com/2020/12/21/politics/bidens-coronavirus-vaccination/index.html.

16 Kate Sullivan and Arlette Saenz, CNN. "Kamala Harris Receives COVID-19 Vaccine Tuesday." *ABC7 San Francisco,* KGO-TV, 29 Dec. 2020, abc7news.com/kamala-harris-covid-vaccine-gets-vaccinated-live-doug-emhoff-coronavirus/9170234/.

17 From Alex Azar.

FIRST STEPS

1 Lisa Schnirring | News Editor | CIDRAP News | Jan 11, 2020. "China Releases Genetic Data on New Coronavirus, Now Deadly." CIDRAP, January 11, 2020. https://www.cidrap.umn.edu/news-perspective/2020/01/china-releases-genetic-data-new-coronavirus-now-deadly.

2 Wallace-Wells, David. "We Had the Vaccine the Whole Time." Intelligencer. Intelligencer, December 7, 2020. https://nymag.com/intelligencer/2020/12/moderna-covid-19-vaccine-design.html.

3 *New York Times*, 3.17.21, A Timeline of the Coronavirus Pandemic, http://www.nytimes.com/article/coronavirus-timeline.html.

4 Adams, Becket. "Yes, Biden Absolutely Did Oppose the China Travel Restrictions and Call Them 'Xenophobic'." Washington Examiner, October 8, 2020. https://www.washingtonexaminer.com/opinion/yes-biden-absolutely-did-oppose-the-china-travel-restrictions-and-call-them-xenophobic.

5 Department of Health and Human Services, Office of the Assistant Secretary for Public Affairs.

6 Lowey, Nita M. "H.R.6074—116th Congress (2019–2020): Coronavirus Preparedness and Response Supplemental Appropriations Act, 2020." *Congress.gov,* 6 Mar. 2020, www.congress.gov/bill/116th-congress/house-bill/6074.

7 "NIH Clinical Trial of Investigational Vaccine for COVID-19 Begins." *National Institutes of Health,* U.S. Department of Health and Human Services, 16 Mar. 2020, www.nih.gov/news-events/news-releases/nih-clinical-trial-investigational-vaccine-covid-19-begins.

8 Loftus, Peter. "WSJ News Exclusive | Drugmaker Moderna Delivers First Experimental Coronavirus Vaccine for Human Testing." *The Wall Street Journal,* Dow Jones & Company, 25 Feb. 2020, www.wsj.com/articles/drugmaker-moderna-delivers-first-coronavirus-vaccine-for-human-testing-11582579099.

9 Kolata, Gina. "What Made New York So Hospitable for Coronavirus?" *The New York Times,* The New York Times, 26 Mar. 2020, www.nytimes.com/2020/03/26/health/coronavirus-nyc-spread.html.

10 Bumsted, Robert. "Hospitals Overflowing with Bodies in US Epicenter of Virus." *AP NEWS,* Associated Press, 31 Mar. 2020, apnews.com/article/virus-outbreak-us-news-ap-top-news-new-york-city-new-york-1b40d68e4969af9fa03e833afd24d709.

11 Kuznia, Robert. "The Timetable for a Coronavirus Vaccine Is 18 Months. Experts Say That's Risky." CNN. Cable News Network, April 1, 2020. https://www.cnn.com/2020/03/31/us/coronavirus-vaccine-timetable-concerns-experts-invs/index.html.

12 Brewster, Thomas. "The U.S. Just Signed A $450 Million Coronavirus Vaccine Contract With Johnson & Johnson." *Forbes,* Forbes Magazine, 30 Mar. 2020, www.forbes.com/sites/thomasbrewster/2020/03/30/the-us-just-signed-a-450-million-coronavirus-vaccine-contract-with-johnson—johnson/?sh=3742f2b42946.

13 "The Fastest Vaccine in History." *Https://Connect.uclahealth.org/,* connect.uclahealth.org/2020/12/10/the-fastest-vaccine-in-history/.

14 "GAO-21-319, Operation Warp Speed: Accelerated Covid-19 ..." Accessed November 11, 2021. https://www.gao.gov/assets/gao-21-319.pdf.

15 Jon Cohen. May. 26, 2020. "Merck, One of Big Pharma's Biggest Players, Reveals Its COVID-19 Vaccine and Therapy Plans." News Flash, May 26, 2020. https://newsflash.one/2020/05/26/merck-one-of-big-pharmas-biggest-players-reveals-its-covid-19-vaccine-and-therapy-plans/.

16 "COVID-19 Clinical Research." *National Institute of Allergy and Infectious Diseases,* US Department of Health and Human Services, www.niaid.nih.gov/diseases-conditions/covid-19-clinical-research.

17 Operation Warp Speed Team Internal Report.

18 Operation Warp Speed Team Internal Report.

19 Lawler, Dave. "America's Vaccine Rollout Has Been among the Best in the World." *Axios,* 21 Feb. 2021, www.axios.com/vaccine-distribution-by-country-us-rollout-doses-9c47fa53–6a2e-4c56–8792-dd31bee34b10.html.

20 "FACT SHEET: 300 Million Shots in 150 Days: The President's COVID-19 Strategy Is Delivering for Americans." *The White House,* The United States Government, 18 June 2021, www.whitehouse.gov/briefing-room/statements-releases/2021/06/18/fact-sheet-300-million-shots-in-150-days-the-presidents-covid-19-strategy-is-delivering-for-americans/.

THE TEAM

1 Robert E. Moffit, Ph.D. "A Federal Health Insurance Exchange Combined with a Public Plan: The House and Senate Bills." The Heritage Foundation. Accessed November 11, 2021. https://www.heritage.org/health-care-reform/report/federal-health-insurance-exchange-combined-public-plan-the-house-and.

2 "Operation Warp Speed Contracts for Covid 19 ... - Congress." Accessed November 11, 2021. https://crsreports.congress.gov/product/pdf/IN/IN11560.

3 Interview with Alex Azar, June 30, 2021.

4 Source would like to remain anonymous.

5 Interview with Alex Azar, June 30, 2021.

6 Interview with Bob Kadlec, June 29 and July 8 , 2021.

7 Interview with Bob Kadlec, June 29 and July 8 , 2021.

8 Interview with Moncef Slaoui, June 16th and 17, 2021.

9 Interview with Moncef Slaoui, June 16 and 17, 2021.

10 Interview with Carlo de Notaristefani, June 17, 2021.

11 "Military Wiki." Military Wiki | Fandom. Accessed November 11, 2021. https://military.wikia.org/wiki/Main_Page.

12 Interview with Peter Marks, July 2, 2021.

13 Interview with Peter Marks, July 2, 2021.

14 Interview with Peter Marks, July 2, 2021.

15 "PN1312—Nomination of Deborah L. Birx for Department of State, 113th Congress (2013–2014)." *Congress.gov,* 2 Apr. 2014, www.congress.gov/nomination/113th-congress/1312.

16 "Birx, Deborah L., M.D." U.S. Department of State. U.S. Department of State. Accessed November 30, 2021. https://2009-2017.state.gov/r/pa/ei/biog/224406.htm.

17 "Who's on the U.S. Coronavirus Task Force." *The New York Times,* The New York Times, 29 Feb. 2020, www.nytimes.com/2020/02/29/health/Trump-coronavirus-taskforce.html.

18 Interview with Peter Marks, July 2, 2021.

19 Interview with Alex Azar, August 7, 2021.

20 Interview with Matthew Hepburn, June 28, 2021.

21 https://en.wikipedia.org/wiki/Francis_Collins.

22 Interview with Francis Collins, July 5, 2021.

23 *National Archives and Records Administration,* National Archives and Records Administration, georgewbush-whitehouse.archives.gov/news/releases/2007/11/20071105–7.html.

24 Interview with Francis Collins, July 5, 2021.

25 Interview with Matthew Hepburn, June 28, 2021.

THE LAUNCH

1 Interview with Moncef Slaoui, June 16 and 17, 2021.

2 Interview with Moncef Slaoui, June 16 and 17, 2021.

3 Interview with Moncef Slaoui, June 16 and 17, 2021.

4 Interview with Peter Marks, July 2, 2021.

5 Interview with Moncef Slaoui, June 16 and 17, 2021.

THE MONEY AND THE SCIENCE

1 Plus, iStock / Getty Images. *Major Health Insurers Agree to Waive Co-Payments for Coronavirus Tests,* 11 Mar. 2020, www.audacy.com/98pxy/blogs/teampxy/major-health-insurers-agree-to-waive-co-payments-for-coronav.

2 "One Hundred Sixteenth Congress of the United States of America." Accessed November 11, 2021. https://www.congress.gov/116/bills/hr748/BILLS-116hr748enr.pdf.

3 Interview with Greg D'Angelo, June 17, 2021.

4 The principle of looking ahead and reasoning back derives from the book *The Art of Strategy: A Game Theorist's Guide to Success in Business and Life* by Avinash L Dixit and Barry J Nalebuff.

5 Clark, Dartunorro. "Pelosi Says No Covid-19 Relief before Election Day, Blames White House for Failing 'Miserably.'" *NBCNews.com,* NBCUniversal News Group, 6 Nov. 2020, www.nbcnews.com/politics/congress/pelosi-says-no-covid-19-relief-election-day-blames-white-n1245016.

6 Patterson, Scott, and Sarah Krouse. "Billions in Federal Covid-19 Testing Funds Still Unspent." *The Wall Street Journal,* Dow Jones & Company, 21 Aug. 2020, www.wsj.com/articles/billions-in-federal-covid-19-testing-funds-still-unspent-11598014623.

7 Interview with Greg D'Angelo, June 17, 2021.

8 Interview with Francis Collins, July 5, 2021.

9 Interview with Francis Collins, July [h], 2021.

10 Interview with Francis Collins, July 5, 2021.

11 Interview with Francis Collins, July 5, 2021.

12 Interview with Francis Collins, July 5, 2021.

13 "John R. Mascola, M.D." *National Institute of Allergy and Infectious Diseases,* U.S. Department of Health and Human Services, www.niaid.nih.gov/about/john-r-mascola-md-bio.

14 Interview with Matt Hepburn, June 28, 2021.

15 "NIH Launches Clinical Trials Network to Test COVID-19 Vaccines and Other Prevention Tools." *National Institutes of Health,* U.S. Department of Health and Human Services, 8 July 2020, www.nih.gov/news-events/news-releases/nih-launches-clinical-trials-network-test-covid-19-vaccines-other-prevention-tools.

16 Interview with Francis Collins, July 5, 2021.

MAKING IT

1 Interview with Carlo de Notaristefani, June 17, 2021.

2 Operation Warp Speed Team Internal Report.

3 Interview with Carlo de Notaristefani, June 17, 2021.

4 Interview with Carlo de Notaristefani, June 17, 2021.

5 Interview with Carlo de Notaristefani, June 17, 2021.

6 "What Is the Defense Production Act?" Council on Foreign Relations. Council on Foreign Relations. Accessed November 11, 2021. https://www.cfr.org/in-brief/what-defense-production-act.

7 "DPAS Training Slides - Bureau of Industry and Security." Accessed November 11, 2021. https://www.bis.doc.gov/index.php/documents/other-areas/strategic-industries-and-economic-security/1615-dpas-training-slides/file.

8 Operation Warp Speed Team Internal Report.

9 Operation Warp Speed Team Internal Report.

10 BerkeleyJr. "Pfizer CEO Says Trump's Executive Orders Overhauling U.S. Drug Pricing Will Upend the Industry." CNBC. CNBC, July 28, 2020. https://www.cnbc.com/2020/07/28/pfizer-ceo-says-trumps-executive-orders-overhauling-us-drug-pricing-will-cause-enormous-destruction.html.

11 Operation Warp Speed Team Internal Report.

12 Operation Warp Speed Team Internal Report.

13 Interview with Carlo de Notaristefani, June 17, 2021.

14 Interview with Carlo de Notaristefani, June 17, 2021.

15 Kramer, Robert. "Emergent BioSolutions CEO: 'Confrontational' Coverage of Vaccine Maker Puts a Target on 'People Doing Good': COMMENTARY." *Baltimoresun.com,* Baltimore Sun, 14 Apr. 2021, www.baltimoresun.com/opinion/op-ed/bs-ed-op-0415-emergent-biosolutions-20210414-g5vfa2rypvgcflqn7x7jouou2u-story.html.

16 Interview with Carlo de Notaristefani, June 17, 2021.

17 Interview with Carlo de Notaristefani, June 17, 2021.

18 Amy Goldstein, Jon Swaine. "Johnson & Johnson to Take Full Control of Its Coronavirus Vaccine Production at Baltimore Plant as AstraZeneca Is Relocated." *The Washington Post,* WP Company, 5 Apr. 2021, www.washingtonpost.com/investigations/emergent-vaccine-jj-baltimore-plant/2021/04/03/25f7ade4–94e2–11eb-9668–89be11273c09_story.html.

19 Interview with Carlo de Notaristefani, June 17, 2021.

20 Letter from the Department of Justice.

21 |, DRJ Editorial Team, and DRJ Editorial Team. "Merck to Help Produce Johnson & Johnson's COVID-19 Vaccine; Barda to Provide Merck with Funding to Expand Merck's Manufacturing Capacity for Covid-19 Vaccines and Medicines • Disaster Recovery Journal." Disaster Recovery Journal. Accessed November 11, 2021. https://drj.com/industry_news/merck-to-help-produce-johnson-barda-to-provide-merck-with-funding-to-expand-mercks-manufacturing-capacity-for-covid-19-vaccines-and-medicines/.

22 Letter from the Department of Justice.

23 Interview with Moncef Slaoui, June 16 and 17, 2021.

24 Interview with Moncef Slaoui, June 16 and 17, 2021.

25 Interview with Moncef Slaoui, June 16 and 17, 2021.

26 Interview with Moncef Slaoui, June 16 and 17, 2021.

SHIPPING IT

1 The New York Times. "See How Vaccinations Are Going in Your County and State." The New York Times. The New York Times, December 17, 2020. https://www.nytimes.com/interactive/2020/us/covid-19-vaccine-doses.html.

2 "Transcript for the CDC Telebriefing Update on COVID-19." *Centers for Disease Control and Prevention,* Centers for Disease Control and Prevention, 26 Feb. 2020, www.cdc.gov/media/releases/2020/t0225-cdc-telebriefing-covid-19.html.

3 Carlsen, Audrey, et al. "How Is The COVID-19 Vaccination Campaign Going In Your State?" *NPR,* NPR, 21 July 2021, www.npr.org/sections/health-shots/2021/01/28/960901166/how-is-the-covid-19-vaccination-campaign-going-in-your-state.

4 "Administration Announces $200 Million from CDC to Jurisdictions for COVID-19 Vaccine Preparedness." *Centers for Disease Control and Prevention,* Centers for Disease Control and Prevention, 23 Sept. 2020, www.cdc.gov/media/releases/2020/p0924–200-million-jurisdictions-covid-19-preparedness.html.

5 Internal Health and Human Services Department Financial office.

6 Operation Warp Speed Team Internal Report.

7 Source chose to be anonymous.

8 Operation Warp Speed Team Internal Report.

9 Operation Warp Speed Team Internal Report.

10 "Covid-19 Vaccination Program Interim Playbook for Jurisdiction Operations. Version 1.0, September 16, 2020." Centers for Disease Control and Prevention. Centers for Disease Control and Prevention. Accessed November 11, 2021. https://stacks.cdc.gov/view/cdc/93806.

11 "Remarks by President Biden on the COVID-19 Response and the Vaccination Program." *The White House,* The United States Government, 6 July 2021, www.whitehouse.gov/briefing-room/speeches-remarks/2021/07/06/remarks-by-president-biden-on-the-covid-19-response-and-the-vaccination-program-6/.

12 Elflein, John. "U.S. Covid-19 Death Rate by State." Statista, November 11, 2021. https://www.statista.com/statistics/1109011/coronavirus-covid19-death-rates-us-by-state/.

13 Aaron Gregg, Douglas MacMillan. "Palantir Goes Public at $10 per Share, Ending 16 Years of Privately Held Secrecy." *The Washington Post,* WP Company, 30 Sept. 2020, www.washingtonpost.com/business/2020/09/29/palantir-public-offering/.

14 "2020–06–11-Mlnc." *CMS,* www.cms.gov/outreach-and-educationoutreachffsprovpart progprovider-partnership-email-archive/2020–06–11-mlnc.

15 Operation Warp Speed Team Internal Report.

DELIVERING IT

1 Interview with Bob Kadlec, June 29 and July 8, 2021.

2 Operation Warp Speed Team Internal Report.

3 Operation Warp Speed Team Internal Report.

4 Interview with Bob Kadlec, June 29 and July [h], 2021.

5 Operation Warp Speed Team Internal Report.

6 "US Faces Nitrile Glove Shortage Ahead of National COVID-19 Vaccination Effort." *CBS News,* CBS Interactive, 7 Dec. 2020, www.cbsnews.com/news/nitrile-glove-shortage-covid-19-vaccine-60-minutes-2020–12–06/.

7 Interview with Peter Marks, July 2, 2021.

8 "Lieutenant General Paul A. Ostrowski ... - Api.army.mil." Accessed November 11, 2021. https://api.army.mil/e2/c/downloads/477917.pdf.

9 Operation Warp Speed Team Internal Report.

10 Operation Warp Speed Team Internal Report.

APPROVING IT

1 "President Trump Addresses White House Summit on COVID-19 Vaccine." *C,* www.c-span.org/video/?507120–1%2Fpresident-trump-addresses-white-house-summit-covid-19-vaccine.

2 "President Trump Addresses White House Summit on COVID-19 Vaccine." *C,* www.c-span.org/video/?507120–1%2Fpresident-trump-addresses-white-house-summit-covid-19-vaccine.

3 Operation Warp Speed Team Internal Report.

4 ABC News. ABC News Network. Accessed November 11, 2021. https://abcnews.go.com/Politics/ trump-vaccine-executive-order-raises-questions-pfizer-offer/story?id=74604381.

5 Vazquez, Maegan, Jim Acosta, and Sara Murray. "Trump Makes Another Largely Symbolic Effort to Combat Coronavirus." CNN. Cable News Network, December 8, 2020. https://www.cnn.com/2020/12/08/politics/trump-vaccine-pfizer-coronavirus-executive-order/index.html.

6 Baker, Peter. "Two Presidents, Two Messages, One Killer Virus." The New York Times. The New York Times, December 9, 2020. https://www.nytimes.com/2020/12/08/us/politics/biden-trump-virus.html.

7 "Deborah Birx and Anthony Fauci Discuss Coronavirus Response: Wsj.com." NewsletterCollector. Accessed November 11, 2021. https://newslettercollector.com/newsletter/deborah-birx-and-anthony-fauci-discuss-coronavirus-response/.

8 Operation Warp Speed Team Internal Report.

9 Interview with Peter Marks, July 2, 2021.

10 "Authorization of Emergency Use of Anthrax Vaccine Adsorbed for Prevention of Inhalation Anthrax by Individuals at Heightened Risk of Exposure Due to Attack With Anthrax; Availability." *Federal Register,* 2 Feb. 2005, www.federalregister.gov/documents/2005/02/02/05–2028/authorization-of-emergency-use-of-anthrax-vaccine-adsorbed-for-prevention-of-inhalation-anthrax-by. interview with peter marks.

11 Center for Biologics Evaluation and Research. "Development and Licensure of Vaccines to Prevent COVID-19." *U.S. Food and Drug Administration,* FDA, www.fda.gov/regulatory-information/search-fda-guidance-documents/development-and-licensure-vaccines-prevent-covid-19.

12 Center for Biologics Evaluation and Research. "Development and Licensure of Vaccines to Prevent COVID-19." *U.S. Food and Drug Administration,* FDA, www.fda.gov/regulatory-information/search-fda-guidance-documents/development-and-licensure-vaccines-prevent-covid-19.

13 "National Vaccine Injury Compensation Program: Rescission of Revisions to the Vaccine Injury Table." *Federal Register,* 22 Apr. 2021, www.federalregister.gov/documents/2021/04/22/2021–08478/national-vaccine-injury-compensation-program-rescission-of-revisions-to-the-vaccine-injury-table.

14 "Development and Licensure of Vaccines to Prevent ... - FDA." Accessed November 11, 2021. https://www.fda.gov/media/139638/download.

15 See, for example, "Are U.S. medical experts being influenced by the Trump Administration? ," *PBS News Hour,* April 26, 2020: "Questions are again being raised about whether the Trump administration is injecting politics into science—and the national pandemic".

16 "Transcript: Pfizer CEO Dr. Albert Bourla on 'Face the Nation," September 13, 2020." *CBS News,* CBS Interactive, www.cbsnews.com/news/transcript-pfizer-ceo-dr-albert-bourla-on-face-the-nation-september-13–2020/.

17 TodayShow. "Pfizer CEO on Coronavirus Vaccine: 'We Will Have an Answer by the End of October.'" *TODAY.com,* www.today.com/video/pfizer-ceo-on-coronavirus-vaccine-we-will-have-an-answer-by-the-end-of-october-91234885714.

18 "An Open Letter from Pfizer Chairman and CEO Albert Bourla." *An Open Letter from Pfizer Chairman and CEO Albert Bourla | Pfpfizeruscom,* www.pfizer.com/news/hot-topics/an_open_letter_from_pfizer_chairman_and_ceo_albert_bourla.

19 "Emergency Use Authorization for Vaccines to Prevent COVID ..." Accessed November 11, 2021. https://www.fda.gov/media/142749/download.

20 "Licensure and Emergency Use Authorization of Vaccines to ..." Accessed November 11, 2021. https://www.fda.gov/media/143352/download.

21 "Licensure and Emergency Use Authorization of Vaccines to ..." Accessed November 11, 2021. https://www.fda.gov/media/143352/download.

22 "Pfizer and Biontech Announce Data from Preclinical Studies OF MRNA-Based Vaccine Candidate Against COVID-19." *Pfizer,* www.pfizer.com/news/press-release/press-release-detail/pfizer-and-biontech-announce-data-preclinical-studies-mrna.

23 "Licensure and Emergency Use Authorization of Vaccines to ..." Accessed November 11, 2021. https://www.fda.gov/media/143352/download.

24 Will Feuer, Nick Wells. "Pfizer CEO Sold $5.6 Million of Stock as Company Announced Vaccine Data That Sent Shares Soaring." *CNBC,* CNBC, 11 Nov. 2020, www.cnbc.com/2020/11/11/coronavirus-vaccine-pfizer-ceo-sold-5point6-million-of-stock-as-company-announced-positive-data.html.

25 "Pfizer and BioNTech Announce Vaccine Candidate Against COVID-19 Achieved Success in First Interim Analysis from Phase 3 Study." *Pfizer Inc.—Investors Overview,* investors.pfizer.com/investor-news/press-release-details/2020/Pfizer-and-BioNTech-Announce-Vaccine-Candidate-Against-COVID-19-Achieved-Success-in-First-Interim-Analysis-from-Phase-3-Study/default.aspx.

26 Axios. "Pfizer CEO Says He Would've Released Vaccine Data before Election If Possible." *Axios,* 9 Nov. 2020, www.axios.com/pfizer-ceo-says-he-wouldve-released-vaccine-data-before-election-if-possible-a4f0c822-bf49–4a04-ac7f-5275c8d895b4.html.

27 Caldera, Camille. "Fact Check: Pfizer Received COVID-19 Vaccine Data after Election Day, Released within Days." *USA Today,* Gannett Satellite Information Network, 19 Nov. 2020, www.usatoday.com/story/news/factcheck/2020/11/18/fact-check-pfizer-received-covid-vaccine-data-after-election-day/6267242002/.

28 Ferguson, Niall, *Doom: The Politics of Catastrophy,* Penguin Press, 2021, . 300.

29 Breuninger, Kevin. "Cuomo and Trump Patch up Their War of Words over Coronavirus as Cases Mount." CNBC. CNBC, March 17, 2020. https://www.cnbc.com/2020/03/17/coronavirus-cuomo-asks-for-federal-help-after-twitter-fight-with-trump.html.

30 LaGrone, Sam. "Trump: Hospital Ship Comfort to Go to New York City, Mercy Set for West Coast Support." USNI News, March 18, 2020. https://news.usni.org/2020/03/18/trump-hospital-ship-comfort-to-go-to-new-york-city-mercy-set-for-west-coast-support.

31 Durkin, Erin. "USNS Comfort Arrives in New York City." Politico PRO, March 30, 2020. https://www.politico.com/states/new-york/albany/story/2020/03/30/usns-comfort-arrives-in-new-york-city-1269589.

32 Cooper, Helene, and Thomas Gibbons-neff. "Navy Hospital Ship Reaches New York. but It's Not Made to Contain Coronavirus." The New York Times. The New York Times, March 30, 2020. https://www.nytimes.com/2020/03/30/us/politics/coronavirus-comfort-hospital-ship-new-york.html.

33 Condon, Bernard. "AP: Over 9,000 Virus Patients Sent into NY Nursing Homes." AP NEWS. Associated Press, February 12, 2021. https://apnews.com/article/new-york-andrew-cuomo-us-news-coronavirus-pandemic-nursing-homes-512cae0abb55a55f375b3192f2cdd6b5.

34 "Trump Approves New York Javits Center to Treat Coronavirus ..." Accessed November 11, 2021. https://www.usnews.com/news/national-news/articles/2020-04-02/trump-approves-new-york-javits-center-to-treat-coronavirus-patients.

35 NewsBreak. "With Empty Beds at the Javits Center and on the Comfort, Uniformed Health Workers Are Going Straight into NYC Hospitals." NewsBreak. NewsBreak, April 14, 2020. https://www.newsbreak.com/new-york/new-york/news/1546756447758/with-empty-beds-at-the-javits-center-and-on-the-comfort-uniformed-health-workers-are-going-straight-into-nyc-hospitals.

36 For example, see "Trump to order priority access to U.S. COVID-19 vaccines for Americans," Reuters, December 7, 2020: "It was unclear why an executive order was needed to ensure that the vaccines would be distributed domestically first, though the order appeared to be designed in part to underscore Trump's "America First" philosophy ahead of the incoming administration of President-elect Joe Biden."

37 "Ensuring Access to United States Government COVID-19 Vaccines." *Federal Register,* 11 Dec. 2020, www.federalregister.gov/documents/2020/12/11/2020–27455/ensuring-access-to-united-states-government-covid-19-vaccines.

38 Pearson, Samantha, et al. "Chinese Covid-19 VACCINE Far Less Effective than Initially Touted in Brazil." *The Wall Street Journal,* Dow Jones & Company, 13 Jan. 2021, www.wsj.com/articles/chinas-sinovac-covid-19-vaccine-is-50–4-in-late-stage-brazil-trials-11610470581.

39 Interview with Garrett Grigsby, July 4, 2021.

40 Interview with Garrett Grigsby, July 4, 2021.

41 Interview with Garrett Grigsby, July 4, 2021.

42 Interview with Garrett Grigsby, July 4, 2021.

43 Operation Warp Speed Team Internal Report.

44 Operation Warp Speed Team Internal Report.

45 Operation Warp Speed Team Internal Report.

SHOWTIME

1 Department of Health and Human Services Daily COVID-19 Report

2 "The Advisory Committee on Immunization PRACTICES' Interim Recommendation for ALLOCATING Initial Supplies of Covid-19 Vaccine—United States, 2020." *Centers for Disease Control and Prevention,* Centers for Disease Control and Prevention, 10 Dec. 2020, www.cdc.gov/mmwr/volumes/69/wr/mm6949e1.htm?s_cid=mm6949e1_w.

3 McElhinny, Brad, et al. "As Supplies Roll into States, West Virginia Could Begin Vaccinating First Nursing Home Residents Tonight." *WV MetroNews,* 14 Dec. 2020, wvmetronews.com/2020/12/14/as-supplies-roll-into-states-west-virginia-could-begin-vaccinating-first-nursing-home-residents-tonight/.

4 Operation Warp Speed Team Internal Report.

5 Hopkins, Jared S., and Dan Frosch. "Pfizer-BioNTech Covid-19 VACCINES Begin Shipping." *The Wall Street Journal,* Dow Jones & Company, 13 Dec. 2020, www.wsj.com/articles/pfizer-biontech-covid-19-vaccines-are-prepped-for-shipment-11607792605.

6 Operation Warp Speed Team Internal Report.

7 Operation Warp Speed Team Internal Report.

8 "Deborah Birx and Anthony Fauci Discuss Coronavirus Response: Wsj.com." NewsletterCollector. Accessed November 11, 2021. https://newslettercollector.com/newsletter/deborah-birx-and-anthony-fauci-discuss-coronavirus-response/.

9 Young, Robin, and Samantha Raphelson. "Trump Administration Had 'No Plan' For COVID-19 Vaccine Distribution, Dr. Michael Osterholm Says." *Trump Administration Had 'No Plan' For COVID-19 Vaccine Distribution, Dr. Michael Osterholm Says | Here & Now,* WBUR, 21 Jan. 2021, www.wbur.org/hereandnow/2021/01/21/biden-covid-19-osterholm.

10 Eban, Katherine. "'A Huge Potential for Chaos': How the Covid-19 Vaccine Rollout Was Hobbled by Turf Wars and Magical Thinking." *Vanity Fair,* 5 Feb. 2021, www.vanityfair.com/news/2021/02/how-the-covid-19-vaccine-rollout-was-hobbled.

11 See, for example, Rosenbaum, Leah. "Pfizer Says It Has Millions Of Vaccine Doses 'Sitting In Our Warehouse'-But Hasn't Been Told Where To Send Them." *Forbes,* Forbes Magazine, 17 Dec. 2020, www.forbes.com/sites/leahrosenbaum/2020/12/17/pfizer-says-it-has-millions-of-vaccine-doses-sitting-in-our-warehouse-but-hasnt-been-told-where-to-send-them/?sh=56ef2786400d.

12 Operation Warp Speed Team Internal Report.

13 Operation Warp Speed Team Internal Report.

14 Department of Health and Human Services, Office of the Assistant Secretary for Public Affairs

15 "CDC Covid Data Tracker." Centers for Disease Control and Prevention. Centers for Disease Control and Prevention. Accessed November 11, 2021. https://covid.cdc.gov/covid-data-tracker/#vaccination-trends.

LESSONS UPON LEAVING

1 "Covid-19 Vaccine Breakthrough Cases: Data from the States." KFF, August 20, 2021. https://www.kff.org/policy-watch/covid-19-vaccine-breakthrough-cases-data-from-the-states/.

2 Interview with Moncef Slaoui, June 16 and 17, 2021.

3 Kennedy, Merrit. "Biden Administration Will Rename 'Operation Warp Speed,' Citing Trump 'Failures.'" *NPR,* NPR, 15 Jan. 2021, www.npr.org/sections/coronavirus-live-updates/2021/01/15/957261530/biden-administration-will-rename-operation-warp-speed-citing-trump-failures.

4 Pager, Tyler, et al. "'It's a Mess': Biden's First 10 Days Dominated by Vaccine Mysteries." *POLITICO,* POLITICO, 2 Feb. 2021, www.politico.com/news/2021/01/30/biden-covid-vaccine-states-463953.

5 Lee, MJ. "Biden Inheriting Nonexistent Coronavirus Vaccine Distribution Plan and Must Start 'from Scratch,' Sources Say." *CNN,* Cable News Network, 21 Jan. 2021, www.cnn.com/2021/01/21/politics/biden-covid-vaccination-trump/index.html.

6 Strassel, Kimberley A. "Opinion | the Obama-Biden Virus Response." The Wall Street Journal. Dow Jones & Company, August 20, 2020. https://www.wsj.com/articles/the-obama-biden-virus-response-11597966209.

7 Hart, Robert. "Biden Promises 100 Million Covid-19 Vaccinations In First 100 Days, Warning That Trump's Approach Would Take 'Years.'" Forbes, Forbes Magazine, 29 Dec. 2020, www.forbes.com/sites/roberthart/2021/12/29/biden-promises-100-million-covid-19-vaccinations-in first 100-days-warning-that-trumps-approach-would-take-years/?sh=383ca7232a97.

8 War in the Persian Gulf Reference Library. . Encyclopedia.com. 25 Oct. 2021 ." Encyclopedia.com. Encyclopedia.com, November 11, 2021. https://www.encyclopedia.com/defense/encyclopedias-almanacs-transcripts-and-maps/sahhaf-mohammed-said-al.

9 "Covid-19 Vaccination Program Interim Playbook for Jurisdiction Operations. Version 1.0, September 16, 2020." Centers for Disease Control and Prevention. Centers for Disease Control and Prevention. Accessed November 11, 2021. https://stacks.cdc.gov/view/cdc/93806.

10 Mitchell, Ellen. "Pentagon Closing Majority of Covid-19 Mass Vaccination Sites." *TheHill,* The Hill, 8 June 2021, thehill.com/policy/defense/557432-pentagon-closing-majority-of-covid-19-mass-vaccination-sites.

11 Higgins-Dunn, Noah. "Trump Covid Vaccine Chief SLAOUI Says Everyone in U.S. Could Be Immunized by June." *CNBC,* CNBC, 1 Dec. 2020, www.cnbc.

com/2020/12/01/trump-covid-vaccine-chief-says-everyone-in-us-could-be-immunized-by-june.html.

12 "Key Things to Know About COVID-19 Vaccines." *Centers for Disease Control and Prevention,* Centers for Disease Control and Prevention, www.cdc.gov/coronavirus/2019-ncov/vaccines/keythingstoknow.html.

13 "Biden Says You May Be Able to Have a Barbecue 'in Your Backyard' by the 4th of July." *CNSNews.com,* cnsnews.com/article/washington/susan-jones/biden-says-you-may-be-able-have-barbecue-your-backyard-4th-july.

14 "Tuskegee Study—Timeline—CDC—Nchhstp." *Centers for Disease Control and Prevention,* Centers for Disease Control and Prevention, 22 Apr. 2021, www.cdc.gov/tuskegee/timeline.htm.

15 Bebinger, Martha, and Blake Farmer. "As COVID VACCINATIONS Slow, Parts of The U.S. Remain Far Behind 70% GOAL." *NPR,* NPR, 5 July 2021, www.npr.org/sections/health-shots/2021/07/05/1013080128/as-covid-vaccinations-slow-parts-of-the-u-s-remain-far-behind-70-goal.

16 Interview with Bob Kadlec, June 29 and July 8th, 2021.

17 "FACT Sheet: 300 Million Shots in 150 Days: The President's COVID-19 Strategy Is Delivering for Americans." *The White House,* The United States Government, 18 June 2021, www.whitehouse.gov/briefing-room/statements-releases/2021/06/18/fact-sheet-300-million-shots-in-150-days-the-presidents-covid-19-strategy-is-delivering-for-americans/.

INDEX